GET ONBOARD:

Walk in the
Shoes of a
Transit Operator

MW01252588

Zia Hussian,

Thank you for your support! I
hope this book inspires you. Dream
big! Never stop believing!

MIROLAND IMPRINT 7

 Canada Council **Conseil des Arts**
for the Arts **du Canada**

 ONTARIO ARTS COUNCIL
CONSEIL DES ARTS DE L'ONTARIO
an Ontario government agency
un organisme du gouvernement de l'Ontario

Canadä

Guernica Editions Inc. acknowledges the support of the Canada Council
for the Arts and the Ontario Arts Council. The Ontario Arts Council
is an agency of the Government of Ontario.

We acknowledge the financial support of the Government of Canada.
Nous reconnaissons l'appui financier du gouvernement du Canada.

GET ONBOARD:

Walk in the Shoes of a Transit Operator

RICHARD LEE

MiroLand
publishers

MIROLAND (GUERNICA)
TORONTO · BUFFALO · LANCASTER (U.K.)
2015

Copyright © 2015, Richard Lee and Guernica Editions Inc.
All rights reserved. The use of any part of this publication,
reproduced, transmitted in any form or by any means, electronic,
mechanical, photocopying, recording or otherwise stored in a
retrieval system, without the prior consent of the publisher is an
infringement of the copyright law.

Connie McParland, series editor
David Moratto, cover and interior book design
Author photo: Salvatore Mirolla
Guernica Editions Inc.
1569 Heritage Way, Oakville, ON L6M 2Z7
2250 Military Road, Tonawanda, N.Y. 14150-6000 U.S.A.
www.guernicaeditions.com

Distributors:
University of Toronto Press Distribution,
5201 Dufferin Street, Toronto (ON), Canada M3H 5T8
Gazelle Book Services, White Cross Mills, High Town, Lancaster LA1
4XS U.K.

First edition.
Printed in Canada.

Legal Deposit—Third Quarter
Library of Congress Catalog Card Number: 2015944688
Library and Archives Canada Cataloguing in Publication

Lee, Richard W., 1985-, author
Get onboard : walk in the shoes of a transit operator / Richard W. Lee.

Issued in print and electronic formats.
ISBN 978-1-77183-129-1 (paperback).--ISBN 978-1-77183-130-7 (epub).--
ISBN 978-1-77183-131-4 (mobi)

1. Lee, Richard W., 1985-. 2. Local transit. 3. Local transit--Employees.
I. Title.

HD8039.M8L44 2015   388.4   C2015-904731-5   C2015-904732-3

You never really know a person
until you understand things
from his or her point of view,
until you climb into his or her skin
and walk around in it.
—Nelle Harper Lee

INTRODUCTION

The Toronto Transit Commission (TTC) is a community of its own with thousands of employees, numerous working sites throughout the Greater Toronto Area (GTA) and thousands of regulations and policies that govern the body of workers. It is a company whose sole purpose is to serve the people of Toronto and the GTA with a means of public transportation. With its rich history in Canada and its long relationship with the people of Toronto, it is truly something to behold. The TTC has been operating in Toronto for over 90 years and it has definitely left a mark in the hearts and minds of millions. What an amazing thought that, in just a few more years, Toronto and the TTC will have been cohabiting for an entire century.

If you fast forward from the beginning of the TTC until now, you can see the vast changes that have occurred within the company. These include changes and additions to TTC landscapes, expansion of transportation routes and the growth of subway and light rail infrastructure. There has been change within the city of Toronto itself with the widespread growth of the population and the increased demand that this has placed on the TTC. Facing such demands, the TTC has had to respond in the way that it operates its business and services to customers. One of the key responses has been to aggressively push towards a more accountable and reliant transit system.

The vision is simple and can be wrapped up in one sentence: the TTC should be a transit system that the people of Toronto can be proud of. But why stop there? Why can't the TTC, among the three largest transit systems in North America, be one that the whole world can admire? Why can't it be a transit system that other transit systems around the world come to emulate? A transit system where others come to seek advice on how to improve their own transit system? On how to build trust and faith amongst the customers? On how to boost morale among its personnel and allow that positive energy to flow out to the public?

The importance of a better customer experience has been the TTC's focal point in recent years. There have been committees created specifically to focus on customer relations. Roles were introduced to work on enhancing the face to face interactions that the TTC personnel have with customers. For it is the customers that ultimately will enhance or damage the reputation of the TTC. There are those who are sceptical about the TTC and view it as a fallen empire. I am sure that we have all heard many complaints, and even voiced a few ourselves. Complaints about service levels, complaints about routing and scheduling adherence, complaints about the price of the fares and complaints about the congestion that TTC vehicles cause. You probably can add to this list yourself.

There are thousands of opinions on how to improve the TTC and its service and there have been many steps implemented towards those goals. However, there is one major issue that has not been discussed that can further change the experience of passengers and the TTC. We can build the best subway systems, purchase new buses and streetcars and place them on the road with the anticipation of attracting more positive vibes. We can offer ample service levels, whether in buses, streetcars, or subways. We can offer the newest technology to dazzle the customers. Having such improvements and upgrades would definitely send off positive signals about the transit system.

Nevertheless, there is something that has been overlooked for many years now and that is as vital or even more vital than all the upgrades and technology to improve customer service. There is an underlying issue that hasn't been widely publicized. This underlying issue has been right in front of our eyes and yet rarely talked about. We need to understand that the relationship between the TTC and the people of Toronto goes well beyond just a transit company reaching out and serving the customers. It goes well beyond a company bending its ear to the people but it has everything to do with people serving people.

It is not the equipment or the vehicles, the newest technology or latest upgrades that serve the customers. It is the TTC operators who are at the frontline. It is the TTC operators that see the customers 365 days a year, 7 days a weeks, 24 hours per day. TTC operators and the public have a deep rooted connection, a relationship so intertwined that there is no way around it. But we rarely hear about the life of a TTC operator and how dealing with the public can have a dramatic impact on that life. There is a common understanding that the TTC is definitely a vital service to the city of Toronto but also the same understanding that city of Toronto is the reason why TTC exists. In short, just as much as the TTC needs Toronto, Toronto needs the TTC.

But what has happened over the years? The emphasis and selling point ha been to improve customer service and their experience with the TTC. Rightly so but solely placing the emphasis on the customer's experience is just one side of the coin. Improving the customer's experience is key but what about improving the TTC operator's experience with the public? If this question is left unanswered, it could be disastrous both for Toronto and the transit system. It is like seeing an apple that is red and shiny on the outside, not one blemish or bruise on it. But when you take a bite, you realize the inside is dark and rotten.

So what does that rotten core represent when we speak about Toronto and the TTC? What issue has been missed for so many years that the apple is starting to decay? The rotten core represents the relationship between passengers and TTC frontline workers. Have you ever thought that, if the relationship between the frontline workers and the public were more of a teamwork, more of an understanding, how the entire transit system would dramatically improve? If you're a transit passenger, have you ever taken into account the difficulties that the operators go through on a daily basis? If you're a transit worker, have you ever taken into account what the public goes through on a daily basis?

The present-day relationship between passengers and TTC operators is, for the most part, one of distrust and discontent. Imagine if the relationship between the public and TTC operators was based more on cooperation and teamwork, rather than unpleasantness and criticism. For the public to have a better experience, and for the TTC to be the leading force in the transit system business, it comes down to the relationship between these parties. It is the customers and the frontline workers who walk hand in hand through the ups and downs, through the bad weather and the good weather, through the valleys and the heights. All those times during subway closures, route diversions, delays in service, accidents, street closures due to parades and festivals, it was the passengers and the TTC operators who shared those experiences. Yet the mending and building better relationships between the two hasn't been a priority.

The reality is that the public at large does not know what a TTC operator actually goes through, and what they actually have to deal with and put up with on a daily basis. There are no articles out that give an accurate or thorough picture of the issues facing operators. There are no platforms or committees that allow TTC operators to share their issues with the public in order for the public to get an understanding of where they are coming from. There is nothing that explains to the public the stresses and pressures of being an operator. I have talked with many operators and the majority of them have said: "If the public only knew ... if the public only knew what we (operators) go through ..." The spark to create this book started with that statement.

There are situations in the lives of operators that have not made the news headlines, newspapers, or in any other media. Have the assaults on TTC operators been covered? Has the press reported incidents of rude passengers spitting on TTC operators? What about the violence and physical assaults that TTC operators have experienced and continue to experience? We're not talking about isolated incidents. Former TTC chairman, Adam Giambrone, has stated:

> *Every day, a TTC driver is assaulted on the job. They are verbally abused. They are threatened. They are punched. They are spat on. Enough is enough. The message is clear: if you commit a crime on one of our vehicles we will catch you, arrest you, charge you and prosecute you. Criminal acts have no place on public transit. Our employees and customers deserve to work and travel in peace. We are committed to ensuring that happens.*

The public rarely hears about an operator getting spat on, or having hot coffee thrown in his or her face for simply following company procedures and policies. The public rarely hears about an operator being threatened with death or personal injury for challenging a customer who chose to refuse payment to board a vehicle. I believe it is time for the voices of the TTC operators to be heard.

Dealing with the general public is always going to be challenging. There will be good and bad experiences due to the fact that not everyone comes from the same ethnic background, speaks the same language, or grew up in the same culture or society. According to Statistics Canada as part of the 2006 census, about half Toronto's population is not native born. In the midst of this great ethnic diversity are the TTC operators, daily exposed to the avalanche of human make up when they step into work for their shift. Yet with over a 500-million ridership per year, and the thousands of operators within the TTC, the primary concern has always been the customers.

Should this be the case? Yes — and no. Yes, because without customers the business cannot survive; no, because the service is being provided by people who are also human beings. We have human beings serving other human beings, and thus the relationship between the two will ultimately dictate the outcome of their experiences. We witness in other fields of work in the public sector the importance of establishing a connection with the community. Firefighters, for example, have such a rapport with the people that they serve, and it is evident that they have such respect from the public. Police departments find it necessary need to build bridges between themselves and those they serve. Programs are created to educate the public about the dangers faced by firefighters and police. This education gives the general public an understanding of the risks, the sacrifices and the dedication exercised by these professionals every day.

The understanding that these two public sectors touch the lives of millions every year through their dedicated service, their devotion and selflessness is well known. So it only makes sense to bring into account the comparison between these two professions and the employees of the TTC transportation sector. I would argue that the TTC frontline workers deal with the same level of public exposure, perhaps more, given the amount of customer interaction. This is not to say that the level of difficulty or danger is the same, but the level of exposure to the general public is the same if not more than these other public sectors experience.

If these other sectors strive for a more harmonious relationship between the public and their frontline workers, then why isn't the TTC and the public striving for such a relationship?

Check out the opinions from the public regarding the TTC through the mainstream media. Whatever the media vehicle, the same message is loud and clear: negative. Simply search the internet and you will be presented with an overwhelming number of articles and videos displaying this negativity. We have all heard about TTC drivers texting while driving, missing designated stops on purpose, leaving buses unattended at the end of the shift despite the fact that there isn't any other operator to take over. We have all seen operators demonstrate poor customer service skills, poor communication skills and a lack of professionalism.

At the same time, we fail to recognize and take into account the majority of operators who take pride in their jobs. We have failed to recogniz that there are operators who come into work day in and day out, working to the best of their abilities and giving their all to the service of the public. Have you ever read in the newspaper about an operator who waited that extra minute for that running customer at the traffic light? What about that operator who gives instructions to that lost passenger even when the operator is off duty? What about that operator who gets the passengers to their destination safely and on time? What about the operator who goes the extra mile in order to provide customer service on a regular basis?

I recalled a scenario about operators going the extra mile and yet, rather than this being recognized, they were ridiculed. There was an Easter parade and roads were closed due to the parade route. Several streetcars had to divert to another street and wait there until the parade was over due to the congestion. As the streetcars were stopped, there was a great confusion created for the motorists all around them. Several operators, upon seeing such confusion, took the initiative in directing traffic so that the vehicles could pass safely. However, as motorists passed by these operators, the majority got angry and cussed, a few were grateful and gave thanks. It wasn't the operators' responsibility to help with the traffic and yet they got treated as if they were dirt by the majority of motorists.

One may say: "Why should the good behavior be recognized, when it is a part of their job description? If the operator doesn't like it, then tough for the operator." This despite the fact directing traffic is not part of an operator's job description. What is really being said here is that we should only recognize operators' bad behavior and forget the good. YouTube is filled with videos of TTC operators, taken by zealous passengers just hoping to gain some sort of notoriety. What an abased feeling the operators are left with knowing that they are always being watched and examined.

I remember standing outside Broadview station one day, with a good friend of mine. We were chatting and feeling amazing about our future with the TTC. It was the end of our shift and, as we were talking, we noticed a woman standing just a few feet away pretending to be on the phone. I noticed that the light for the recording feature on the phone was switched on and I realized that she was trying to capture us speaking. It actually made me feel like a criminal, as if I was doing something wrong. I felt guilty for standing around after my shift talking to a colleague.

The TTC has had this "two ears wide open" attitude towards the public for more than 90 years. The voice of the public has dramatically strengthened and has driven changes and modifications to the TTC's operating system, policies and way of conducting business. This open ear arrangement has given preferential treatment to the opinions of the public over the frontline workers, a very one sided environment. It has given the public a microphone to scream out their complaints and problems, especially to those with a TTC logo. It feels like having that logo on your shirt gives people a license to say whatever they want whether its good or bad, constructive or damaging. But the frontline workers' lips need to be sealed or there are consequences to be paid.

We all have our stories. We have all had a negative experience relating to the TTC. It starts from one bad experience, probably a long time ago, and the seed is planted in fertile ground. The bad experience could be anything: having to take a shuttle bus due to subway closures; waiting an extended amount of time for the streetcar; sitting in the subway train underground motionless when there is a service delay. It could be due to the fact that during a winter storm the bus that usually comes every 5 minutes took more than 30 minutes to arrive and as a result you are now late for work. Or the idea of fares being increased might have a negative impact on the way you feel about the TTC. Or that the operator who was supposed to leave at a certain time, left early and therefore you missed your connections on other routes. Or that you see 3 to 4 buses in a row but none of them are coming your way.

That bad experience has created an image in your mind and set in motion the negative attitude you have towards the TTC.

With your own experience and hearing about other stories through social media, it is natural to blame the ones you see the most, the frontline workers. And it is these frontline workers, the TTC operators who get the abuse, negativity and verbal diatribes. Despite the fact they often have little control over the situation, the frontline workers get an earful from angry customers. If you look at the situation in terms of a marriage, for more than 90 years the TTC and Toronto have been wed. Now it appears that the marriage has gone sour. For the longest time the public and the frontline workers of the TTC have had an unhappy, unappreciated, rocky relationship at best. It is time to seek some marriage counselling.

What will you gain from reading this book? It is all about seeing, walking and understanding that TTC operators are human beings. You will read first hand stories and statements from operators who have actually lived through such experiences. You will read about how dealing with the public can literally affect a person's life, attitude and even their view of themselves. You will appreciate and understand the deteriorating connection between the people of Toronto and TTC operators and how it really does influence what type of experience each party will have of the other. I have also included my own story, my journey from the beginning of my TTC career to the present. You will have the opportunity to see the pitfalls, the temptations, the mind-battles, and the triumphs I have gone through to get here. At the same time, I am not alone in this. My story is similar to that of many other operators.

This book is dedicated to the Toronto Transit Commission frontline workers who have been giving their all in order to serve the public. This book is dedicated to those who are presently serving the public but also those who are retired. All you did for the TTC and for Toronto should not be forgotten. This book is dedicated to the frontline operators all over the world. You truly make a difference. This book is dedicated to the thousands of operators who have been physically assaulted or verbally abused for simply doing their jobs. The world needs to know what you truly go through by walking in the shoes of an operator.

I am passionate about getting the awareness out that transit operators are human beings and that as such they deserve to be treated with respect. I truly believe that, as we begin to change the core of the apple, the apple itself will begin to look and taste better.

WALKING IN THE SHOES OF A TRANSIT OPERATOR I

Author: *Do you think that the public really know what TTC operators go through?*

Operator 1: *It is pretty sad but the reality is that most passengers have no clue what we go through for many think it is just a case of driving from point a to point b. When some see us they think: "What an easy job." That we just sit and drive. But dealing with the public is no walk in the park. I saw a driver break down in tears after being yelled at by a passenger. There is one driver that I know personally who is dealing with stress related issues because of the demands of the public. If the public only knew what we face I totally believe they would be more understanding about what happens with the operators.*

Operator 2: *I have heard a lot of people say that transit operators are just lazy people who sit on their ass all day and do nothing. But little do they see the impact we truly have on people's lives on a daily basis and the sacrifices we endure in our own lives.*

Operator 3: *I don't think that the public at large knows about all the incidents, the abuse, the mental stresses of this job and what the operators face on a continual basis. I would say it is the verbal abuse that would be the number one choice of weapon used by angry customers. But just imagine if I go to the bank day after day and verbally harass the teller. How would the teller feel as a human being? It is the same with TTC operators. The public doesn't understand that we are human beings too.*

Operator 4: *There has been times when after listening to angry customers for whatever reasons, that there have been other customers that come up to me and say how he or she doesn't know how I can do this job. There have been many customers who understand that not everything that happens with the TTC is our fault. So I have to say that there are some who really understand what we go through but the majority of customers don't or just don't care.*

Author: *How do you feel when you know that the public can literally say anything to you whether negative or positive without being held accountable?*

Operator 5: *It is really unfortunate knowing that being employed by TTC is like having a target on your back for the public to throw verbal axes at. I remember after work one evening being at the local grocery store still being in my TTC uniform. In the process of paying for my groceries, a gentleman behind me began to tell me everything he thought was wrong with TTC and kept going for the whole time I was gathering my food.*

Operator 6: *I love my job and I have nothing but respect for this company, but what I believe is missing is the accountability of the public for the things that they do and say to operators. TTC is doing an amazing job now of charging unruly passengers, and it is good to know that the organization is starting to see what operators have to deal* with. *Sometimes it feels as if we (operators) are human punching bags for the public to use at will. It is sometimes hard not to say what is on my mind when a customer starts to scream at me.*

Operator 7:   *I know it is hard not to take it personally, but usually all it takes is one person's rude comment to throw your whole day into the gutter. I know it shouldn't be like that but that is the reality. I remember I was giving directions to an elderly lady who was confused with the diversions the buses were taking due to a closure. It took longer than I assumed and I heard a voice coming from back of the bus saying: "Just drive, you bus driver."*

Operator 8:   *I have had many experiences from customers who have said many wonderful things to me but also many customers have said nasty things. On this job you really got to take the negative words by passengers with a grain of salt. I give much respect for the TTC operators around the city because, with the verbal attacks that many get, they still act in a professional way.*

Author: *How do you feel about working for the public these days and do you think times have changed regarding how the passengers treat TTC operators?*

Operator 9:   *What is sad about the passengers these days (and I have been driving for a long time) is that common courtesy is no longer the norm now but it is looked upon as abnormal. Before it was common to receive a thank you from passengers. Nowadays the ratio is so low that sometimes*

I might as well be a robot. There were even days picking up and dropping off customers when I didn't receive a single "thank you." By the end of the day you sometimes can feel the same as a piece of dirt.

Operator 10: *I have 20 plus years on the job and I would say that the manners and attitude of people have definitely changed. I am not saying that all passengers have this negative vendetta towards the TTC, but certainly what I am saying is that respect from passengers towards operators is on a slippery slope.*

Operator 11: *We are definitely living in a day and age where the mentality is all about me, myself and I. But there are customers who still have manners and common courtesy. It is rare to see, but they do exist.*

Author: *Why do you think it is important for the public to get a more positive view of TTC operators?*

Operator 12: *The public needs to know that we are human beings as well. We are mothers, fathers, sisters and brothers, not robots. The view of TTC operators has gone down simply because of the increase in videos and pictures taken by people that present only a part of the story to the media and public. Images and videos are portraying operators as the aggressor or the antagonist without really having the full truth. It is unfortunate that there are people out there who thrive from getting their 30 seconds of fame.*

Operator 13: *It is very important that the public changes their outlook on operators especially because it is not like they can avoid operators or try to avoid them. We see them every day, sometimes twice a day and yet there is such a wall between us and the public. There needs to be something done to change the attitude that the public has with regards to the TTC but more importantly the operators.*

Operator 14: *There are thousands of TTC operators and it is very disturbing that the majority of the attention is on the ones who are unprofessional. We (operators) know the ones that just don't care about their jobs, but if you ask them to quit, they won't. But at the same time there are so many operators who excel at customer service and they hardly ever get noticed. That is a shame.*

Operator 15: *It is so important to get the awareness out there that being a TTC operator is much more than just driving for we deal we so many things on any given shift. We are serving the public daily and it would be nice to know that the public views us as humans not just an object.*

Operator 16: *It is hard not to go on social media and type the letters TTC without coming across some form of negative statements. But what would be such a relief is for the passengers to see what really happens in the life of a TTC operator. There needs to be something that gives out such awareness.*

Transformation is a process, and as life happens there are tons of ups and downs. It's a journey of discovery, there are moments on mountaintops and moments in deep valleys of despair.

—Rick Warren

CHAPTER 1

─────

BEGINNING
OF THE JOURNEY

Growing up in Toronto as the youngest of three brothers, and a home devastated by the divorce of my parents, it was hard for me to find my niche. When I was six, it was obvious my parents were having marital problems and within a few years they divorced. My brothers, Robert the oldest and Ryan the middle child, spent a lot of their time together as they had similar interests. My mother was so distraught with the divorce that she spent the majority of her time in her room watching television. Many nights, I wanted to share with her things that were in my heart, but I held back when I heard her crying in her room.

I handled the breaking of the family and the feeling of being unwanted by isolating myself in the basement of the house. I took all of my belongings from the bedroom that I had shared upstairs with Ryan, and took refuge in the "cave" of the house. Many nights I spent sleeping on the floor with four to five blankets covering me to try and keep warm, especially during the winter months. Coming from school I would go straight to the basement and spend

the majority of my time reading books, mainly on character building and leadership.

Despite the fact that my home life was not ideal, school was
my biggest fear. I developed a severe stutter as a child, and grew
up having others stare and laugh at me. Speaking in front of others
whether in groups or individually was more terrifying than the
idea of dying. One particular incident put a dark cloud over my life
and cast a negative experience in me as a young child. I was in the
4th grade and it was the first day of school. Though I was very
excited to see my friends from the previous year, I was also extremely nervous about the beginning of the class. For it was at the
beginning of the class that the teacher would always request us to
stand up and say our name and then say something about ourselves.
Into the classroom I went, sitting in the back and trying to hide so
as not to be spotted by the teacher. I could hear my heart pounding
inside my chest so loud that it drowned out all the noise around
me. The classroom started to fill up with students and, as the commotion simmered down, the teacher got up and said:

"Let's start off with the introduction and I want everyone to
tell the class a little bit about themselves as well."

Starting with the front row, one by one each student introduced themselves and told the class what they did in the summer
and how they were excited about the coming year. The time was
coming for me to give my name and the closer it got to me the
louder my heart pounded. My palms were sweaty, my throat was
dry and the realization of my having a hard time even saying my
name aloud was vivid. There was no way out of it. There was no
excuse. I turned my head to listen to the boy beside me give his
name and say something about himself. The time came when the
classroom was staring at me and, with every eye was on me, the
teacher said:

"It is your turn, son. Tell us your name, how your summer went and one thing about yourself."

I slowly gazed across the classroom and saw the eagerness of the students listening to me. I saw the teacher and I could tell that she was wondering why I was taking longer than all the other students. I started to rub my hands together trying to wipe away the sweat that accumulated on them. I took a deep breath and opened my mouth ...

"My name is Rrrrrr ..."

I stopped and paused. Putting my head slightly lower to my desk I opened my mouth again.

"My name is R ... Rrrrr ... Rrrrr ..."

The classroom erupted with smirks and laughter. I tried once again and the same blockage hindered me from speaking my name. The noise of the classroom got a little louder and I could see on the teacher's face the frustration she had with me and the noise created. I mustered up the courage to give it another try but before I could even open my mouth this time, the teacher interrupted me and told the class to be quiet.

"Richard, why are you causing trouble? Go stand outside the classroom please."

I rose from my seat and feeling ashamed and humiliated, packed up my stuff and stood outside the classroom. Such experiences happened often throughout my childhood and such experiences created in me a sense of despair.

To counter the rejection that I had felt at home and at school, I had a secret place where I went during the night time that was very special to me. Behind my house was a large forest with a path that led down to an open field and a small creek. My alarm would wake me up around 1:00 am and I would quietly leave my home to head towards this open field. Sneaking outside, my heart would be filled with joy knowing that I would soon be at my secret place and be all alone. When you stood at the entrance of the path at the top of the hill, there would literally be nothing but darkness. The tall trees would cover the night sky and prevent the stars from giving any sort of light to the path. You could see nothing in front of you or beside you and all you heard were noises from the bushes or the rustling of the trees all around you.

I must confess that some nights I was filled with fear, heading down that hill as a young boy, but the desire to spend time sitting at the creek in the open air looking at the stars was worth the fear. Finally reaching the bottom of the hill, stepping away from the darkness of the forest and into my sacred place, it would appear as if the curtains from a window had been pulled open because the light would suddenly come shining through from the stars and moon. There was a lovely small creek between two pieces of land and an old bridge that gave a connecting pathway for the two. Along the side of the creek were large rocks and boulders giving me a perfect place to sit and admire the beauty of the night. I would sit there for hours and think about life and allow my imagination to soar as high as the stars. It was as if being there gave me a sense of peace, a sense of innocence and a sense of calmness in my soul. I hated leaving that place of tranquillity to face the realities of the world. However, it wasn't all negative.

Growing up in a neighbourhood filled with kids was the greatest time in my life. We used to play any type of sport imaginable. My house was the rallying point and from there we would branch off to our destination to start whatever activity we came up with. One summer day during school break, struggling for something to do, we decided to watch a wrestling match. As young boys the adrenaline started to rise, so much so that we began our own wrestling matches—on my mother's bed! We each picked our

World Wrestling Federation characters, created the costumes for each other and had the entrance song that resembled the character we had chosen to imitate. We even recorded it. The stage was set, the wrestlers ready and the match was on. It was quite the sight. Just imagine 10 young boys wrestling and fighting on the bed without a care in the world. We ended up breaking the majority of the things that were in my mother's bedroom. The look on our faces was as if everyone had seen a ghost.

All the other kids left, safe in the knowledge that the impending doom from my mother would not rest on them, but on me and my two brothers. Ryan and I looked to Robert to fix everything. My oldest brother was known to be the handyman in the family growing up, so Ryan and I were given the assignment of cleaning and making sure that the room was tidy. Robert managed to fix everything and the room looked as if no one had used it. When my mother's car pulled up to the driveway, my brothers and I yelled, "MIC, MIC" (mom is coming). Hearing the keys jingling at the door, all three of us ran to our own rooms pretending to be sons of perfection.

After my mother made known that she was at home, she skirted up to her room to watch television. I breathed a sigh of relief. I didn't hear my mother say anything for more than 20 minutes. But the silence broke when all three of our names were called and we were instructed to come to her room at once. I was the last to enter and noticed that the room really looked impeccable. I thought that we had got away with the wrestling match because I couldn't see anything in that room that was out of the ordinary. Until she pressed play on the VCR. The entire wrestling match that we had recorded was playing on the television screen in front of us! We forgot to remove the video after all the kids had watched it. Busted!

I loved the neighbourhood kids. Though we got into all kinds of trouble, it brought a sense of family into my life. I noticed quickly that the only way to be truly accepted and welcomed in that neighbourhood was to play basketball and to play it well. Being a small boy desperately in need of acceptance, I gave myself over to the idea of becoming the best basketball player in the neighbourhood. I dedicated countless hours a day to improving my basketball skills and abilities. I transformed my room in the basement into a basketball obstacle course by using all sorts of items and furniture in order to create greater challenges for me with the ball.

By the time I was 10 years old, my skills and abilities in the game had grown so much that the dream of playing professionally was born in my heart. It was my only desire, a burning passion to someday step onto the hardwood court and live out my dream. I would practice my dribbling and shooting skills every day, even missing classes at school. Training at night was the best teacher to me because just the thought that everyone else was sleeping fuelled me to push and train harder. Soon around the neighbourhood I was considered to be a top notch player and the dream about playing professionally grew larger each passing day. It was either playing professionally or nothing at all for I had no other goal or prize to pursue in my life.

Throughout my early teen years I travelled extensively in the United States to various basketball exposure and training camps in order to get some sort of attention from coaches at reputable colleges. I taped every game that I played during my tenure in high school and sent the tapes all over the country, trying to get some sort of break and a chance to play. I used every cent of the little income I had earned from my job at McDonald's to fund my travelling expenses and the sending out of video tapes to universities. The cost didn't matter to me. I wanted to get a scholarship more than anything in life. One by one letters from the colleges and universities I'd approached came — letters of rejection. When my mother would call and say that I had mail from a certain university regarding my basketball tape, I was filled with excitement. But that joy would quickly turn into disappointment when I opened it and read that my skills weren't needed at that time at that particular university.

Over the course of several months and after realizing that I had exhausted all the colleges and universities, I decided to email and send tapes to as many basketball camps in the United States as possible. Again one by one recruiters from these camps already had the players that fit my style of basketball. Until one day I received an email from a coach in Jacksonville, Florida. His name was Grayson Marshall. He wrote me a beautiful email and said that he would love to give me the chance to showcase my talent at his upcoming basketball exposure camp. He mentioned how he would also invite me to stay in his home with his family and give me free board during the time I was in Florida. Of course when I my mother, she investigated it thoroughly. After a few weeks she was quite satisfied to let me go.

Getting off the plane that sunny morning was scary. I was alone and had no clue who this man was or what he looked like. But I had such a calmness in my heart that everything would work out perfectly. After picking up my bags from the luggage conveyor and walking towards the exit, I couldn't really see anyone looking around as if to search for someone. But when I was walking out into the crowd a little further, I saw a big smile from this bald well-built black man. I walked up to him and there was an instant connection between us, like a father and son relationship.

We drove to his home and I was introduced to his lovely family and they took me in as their own. Daily I was working out with Coach Marshall in his gym as early as 4:00 am, working on different drills and practicing my ball skills. Off the court, I was exposed to much more than basketball. I witnessed the love and tenderness that the Marshall family shared with each other. It made me again think about the lack of togetherness in my own family life and my lack of close friends.

Travelling a lot as a young teen made it hard for me to establish strong relationships, and I was starting to feel that void in my heart. Despite these feelings of loneliness, I pressed on towards my goal of getting a basketball scholarship at this exposure camp. I was 17 years old at the time and, as a result of the camp, interest came from the recruiter from the University of Tennessee at Martin. It was arranged that I would attend junior college for a year and then would be recruited to this particular university. My dreams and goals were starting to turn into reality and off I went to the junior college.

It was a very lonely time, and I arrived at a place in my life where all I wanted to do was to have quality relationships, just someone to love me. All of my youth, I had been travelling and trying to chase after my dream but there was a yearning in my heart for friends and connections. I was getting homesick and, despite my growing success within the college, I woke up one morning and decided I didn't want to play basketball anymore. I walked into the head coach's office and told him that I wanted to go home. He pleaded with me to continue, to stick it out. But his words fell on deaf ears.

I wasn't really thinking about my dream at the time. I wasn't really thinking about basketball and my future. All that was going through my mind was the emptiness in my heart. The need to be wanted, the need to be loved was too overwhelming for me, and, no matter what the coach said, my heart was not with basketball anymore. I packed up my stuff and headed back home to Toronto, to my family. I didn't realize at the time what a devastating mistake it was, one that would haunt me for many years to come.

Almost a year had passed since I'd returned home when the realization of foregoing my childhood dream crushed my spirit. Thoughts of regret rushed through my heart, thoughts of being a failure in life consumed and overwhelmed me. There was no returning to the junior college, no more interest from colleges or universities and it caused me to go into a deep depression. From time to time my family and friends would remark that I could have played in the NBA if I had stayed. It was like having a demon inside my mind. At the age of 20 I was unmistakably at my ultimate low. I felt as if I had nothing to give to the world, as if I had no other skills or abilities. I felt as if I was not a man. I didn't finish college or university; I hardly had a really connection with my family and very few friends in Toronto.

Scrambling around in my mind and doing some soul searching, I had to come up with another plan for my life. Some other goal to strive for, some other purpose in my life to pursue. But I came up with nothing. Some nights the tears from my eyes soaked my pillow and the flies on the walls heard my wallows. I saw some of my friends already at university. Some had full time jobs. Some had cars and girlfriends. It hurt me to compare my life to theirs. In my own eyes I was an utter failure, a man who quit when the going got tough.

I made a vow never to quit at anything ever again. There wasn't a lot I could do regarding getting a high paying job, since I didn't have schooling or any particular job experience to fall back on. So I went back to the same McDonald's where I had worked previously. The owner welcomed me back with open arms and I was glad to be a part of the crew would again. I was a cook for a while, and during my time at the grill my mind would again be the battlefield of wars fought with myself on how I was on my way to becoming a basketball star, and now I was working at a fast food restaurant flipping burgers.

I decided to change my outlook about my job and about my life. I needed a positive direction. I challenged myself every day to try to stay positive. If I was going to be a cook for McDonald's, I made up my mind to be the best cook that McDonald's had ever had. I started to see every shift as an opportunity to grow my character, to improve on my interpersonal skills and to focus on being a better man. Working with such a mindset started to pay off as it was apparent that I was gaining the favour of my boss and other store managers at that restaurant. The owner offered me a manager's job, and I gratefully accepted.

During my time as a manager at McDonald's, I fell in love with Emma. We met at the local church where my mother had taken us since our youth. Emma had this grace about her that was unmatched by any other woman I knew at the time. I was 21 years old, with no formal education, no real idea about a career plan—and working at McDonald's. She didn't care about that. She loved me for who I was as a person with all my flaws and weaknesses. We spent all of our free time together, like peas in a pod, and we both felt like it was us against the world.

At the same time, the flame of becoming something more in life started to grow within me. I knew it would have been impossible to see myself as a man if I had settled with being a manager at McDonald's. All I wanted was to make this woman proud of me and even more proud to say that she was with me. After hearing my desires to advance my life and career, my colleagues at McDonald's as well as others I knew suggested that I apply for a position at the TTC.

I have been working there for over 20 years now. Richard, it's a great job.

Richard, you know that the TTC is hiring and you have been working at McDonald's for a while now. Why don't you just give it a try?

All you need is to get your foot in the door and you can do whatever you want within that company. The TTC is a very reputable company to work for and I know you would do great there.

After listening to my friends about the benefits of working for the TTC and how it would be a great career choice, I was fully convinced that it would be an amazing accomplishment for me if I got the job there. I tasked myself with pursuing ways to acquire information on being a TTC operator. Wasting no time, I put my resume together, put on my only suit and made my way down to the TTC employment centre. Walking into the building was a thrilling experience. I had read about the history of the TTC and the background on how much the company had grown. As I walked into the employment office, several others were filling out applications. I knew that, despite the negative perception about being a "bus driver," this job was highly sought after. I placed my resume in the tray and walked out with great anticipation and zeal about becoming an operator.

That night, I told my mother I had done but didn't tell anyone else, not even my girlfriend. As the months went by, my relationship with Emma had grown into something very special. But I didn't feel like a man because I was working at a place where I knew that my potential wasn't really being used. However, the possibility of working for the TTC faded after a while because I thought that my resume had perhaps not made the grade. I started to look at other careers and applied to the Toronto Police Services, but to no avail.

During this time of searching for self, searching for a career and trying to establish myself, I was reading books on leadership and the character of the soul. At work I tried to lead by example, in the way that I dressed, the way that I spoke to the customers, the way that I conducted myself and related myself to the team that I was managing. Every morning I would wash the windows and clean the outside of the restaurant despite the fact that there wasn't anyone inside yet. One morning, after the usual peak hour rush, I was washing the windows when I felt my phone vibrating. The person introduced himself as a TTC representative. He wanted to conduct a phone interview. By this time, I had totally forgotten about the TTC application and the position that I had applied for, so it took me a few moments to recollect what he was talking about.

After composing myself and understanding that this one phone call could change the course of my life, I answered every question to the best of my ability. After hanging up the phone and feeling quite satisfied about my answers, I felt as if I was already in possession of the TTC employee pass. One day, a few weeks later, after returning home from work, my mother called me into the kitchen and handed me an envelope. It was from the TTC. I slowly opened the envelope and, taking the letter between my fingers, I placed it on the table face down. My mother looked at me and said: "Whatever the letter says, I am very proud of you."

I took the letter from the table, turned it over and read the first sentence. My eyes swelled up and got a little watery as I knew that my life would change for the better.

Congratulations you have been selected in the recruitment process ...

When I read the first few words, I dropped the letter and gave my mother a huge hug, for I knew that I was one step closer to becoming an operator. Within the letter there were details: a date, time and location where the initial recruiting phase would begin, the orientation.

WALKING IN THE SHOES OF A TRANSIT OPERATOR II

Author: *What was life like before you worked for the TTC?*

Operator 1:   *Before the TTC, I had several jobs. Two and three jobs just to make ends meet. It was very hard to see the light at the end of the tunnel but who knew a simple application could change all of that?*

Operator 2:   *The TTC has been a great company to work for, despite what anyone says about it. I worked construction for many many years and I would say that is a lot harder than what we as operators are doing. I had to work more than 14 hours per day usually to keep food on the table for my family. A friend of mine who worked for the TTC told me to apply, and I am glad I did.*

Operator 3:   *It was tough before the TTC, for I was married and had two children and for many years we survived on one income. My wife used to pick up odd jobs here and there but it was definitely a struggle month to month.*

Operator 4:   *I actually started this job as a summer student so I was very fortunate to get this job at such a young age. But I could imagine what life would have been like if I had not had this job as an operator.*

Operator 5:   *I remember getting that phone call, the over the phone interview. I was so nervous. At that time, even though I had finished university with a good degree, I wasn't successful in landing a decent job. It was so tough out there* to find a good job but luckily that phone rang and I passed that stage of the process.

Operator 6: I had many jobs before working for the TTC—even my own business. But at the end of the I was always worrying. I was always thinking about the businesses that I ran and over time my health started to decrease. Work was literally destroying my life. I was stretching myself too thin. I was more than willing to give it all up to work for the TTC.

Operator 7: I think life for me was normal. My family and I were actually doing very well but it was the whole security aspect of my job at that time that was not really stable. However, I was greatly humbled when I got this job over 10 years back—and I still am.

Operator 8: I was working for a large corporation before working for the TTC and I must say, despite what others may say about the company, it is definitely true in my own experience that the TTC is one of the best companies to work for.

Operator 9: Before working for the TTC as an operator, I actually had my own business but it was very difficult balancing life and work. I was always on call and took a lot of work home. So to get a job where I can just work my hours and not worry about work after work is a great privilege for me. TTC has been good for me and I am so looking forward to spending all my working years with this company.

It's best to have failure happen early in life.
It wakes up the phoenix bird in you
so you rise from the ashes.

—Anne Baxter

CHAPTER 2

———

THINGS ARE LOOKING UP

Finally I could see a bright future ahead of me, the light at the end of the tunnel. After realizing that I couldn't go back to the States and fulfill my basketball scholarship and, after losing all sense of self, it was this letter that brought hope and gave me something to strive for. But not just that. I was also thinking about how working for the TTC could advance my relationship with Emma. I saw her as a wife, someone I could be with for the rest of my life and I thought that having a job with the TTC would enable me to take care of her in many other ways than I could do as a manager at McDonald's.

On the day of the orientation, I wore the same suit as on the day I handed in my application. There were hundreds of people lined up waiting to enter the hotel where the proceedings would take place. I remember sitting in the auditorium, filled with applicants all dressed in their best attire waiting for a spokesperson from the TTC to tell us more about the job. I was 22 years old and full of energy and excitement. I kept thinking how thankful I was to even get this far in the recruitment process.

As the meeting was about to commence I noticed that a few people were not allowed to enter because they had missing documents and inadequate information. I questioned why people would take such an opportunity so lightly and not have the necessary materials. I knew that there must have been thousands who applied and thousands who were rejected. I was humbled to make it this far. When it was time to start the presentation, the chatter among the audience came to a stop as the TTC representative walked towards the front of the room. We all looked intently forward, listening with open ears in order to learn as much as we could about this job. I wanted know everything that being a TTC operator entailed, the ins and outs, the good and the bad.

About five minutes into his speech, the back door opened and a young lady rushed into the room and sat down at an empty seat. The spokesperson discussed many things about the job: the scheduling of the work; how it wasn't a nine-to-five type of job; how it was strictly shift work. He discussed the importance of customer service, the importance of being on time, the importance of representing yourself as an operator in a professional manner. He went through the benefits and pay of the job and all of the perks, leaving nothing out.

He spent as much time telling us about the negative aspects of the job, as he did the positive. Many people in the room may have been thinking about the job as if it was something easy to do. But hearing what the job entails caused many to have second thoughts about pursuing such a career path. At the end of the presentation, a small test was issued, to be completed within a set time. The same lady who came late at the beginning of the orientation was the first to finish. She walked proudly up to the front of the room and handed her paper to the spokesperson. After she exited the room, he took her paper and ripped it in half. I always assumed the reason for this was because she came in late. This wasn't something to play around with. This company meant business. After completing that small quiz, there was an assignment that needed to be done in preparation for those who would go on to the next stage of the recruitment process—the panel interview.

The assignment was job shadowing. The potential candidate had to shadow an operator on the job and ask him or her about the job and about their own experiences. It was an excellent way to get a better snapshot of the life of a TTC operator. There was a list that was given out at the orientation of the specific routes and questions that needed to be answered. Some questions were the name of the route, the time of the day, the number of the bus and run number. There were also questions more related to the operators themselves. It was apparent that the process of becoming an operator was no easy task and, looking back at what needed to be done, I have nothing but respect for all those who endured and passed this process. Emma at this time was no longer just a friend whom I loved. We were officially in a relationship. She encouraged me throughout the whole process and came with me on every assignment.

The homework required the candidates to perform 10 different interviews with various operators from the bus division, streetcar and subway. We rode around Toronto from the east to the west trying to conduct these in interviews with different operators from different routes and areas. One of the requirements was to interview an operator during the midnight shift on a streetcar route. Leaving the midnight interview until the end was a tough one because of the schedule that Emma and I had with our current jobs. But off we went into the night, to gather the information to finish the assignment. She parked her car at the Eaton town centre parking lot, and I knew that she was so tired and was starting to fall asleep. I didn't want her to come with me, because I knew it would take a while, so I told her to get some rest in the car and I would be back as soon as I could.

After I left the car, she moved over to the passenger seat and covered herself with a blanket. Looking back and seeing her so sleepy gave me a heavy heart. She was here because of me and I knew that with all of the sacrifice there would be nothing that would stop me from getting this job. I got on the streetcar and, because I was the only one on it, I took my time asking the questions. After an hour or so, I left the streetcar operator to continue and I made my way back to the car. I found Emma fast asleep. I leaned over and whispered in her ear: "Thank you, baby, we are all done."

I knew at that moment that she was the woman for me, and that I wanted to marry her. She had done so much for me and I wanted to do all that was in my power to show her that she was appreciated and loved.

Weeks went by without hearing from the TTC until one day I received a letter in the mail. Without opening the letterI totally knew without a shadow of a doubt that I had passed the test and was advancing to the next stage of the recruitment process. I opened the letter to find I had been accepted and was given the date for a panel interview. I was more than excited because I was one step closer in becoming a TTC operator. As previously mentioned, I am not the greatest orator but wasn't going to let anything stop me from achieving my goals. As the interview time approached, I took time every morning to visualize myself before the panel speaking with clarity and confidence.

The time came for the interview and, putting on the same suit again, I was beaming with confidence. Sitting on that chair waiting for the TTC representative to come and begin the interview, thoughts of my past began to surface. Thoughts about my childhood and how being a stammering child evoked fear in my heart every time a speaking engagement was heading my way. But this time instead of dwelling upon such fearful thoughts of being laughed at, or fearful thoughts of feeling embarrassed, I made up my mind to go in with more confidence than I have ever had. I knew at this point in my life that I had come a long way since I was that frightened young boy sitting in that classroom.

I entered and left that interview with nothing to regret because I gave it all that I had in me. I was extremely humbled even to get this far in the recruiting process with the TTC. A few weeks passed, waiting for any word from the TTC, until finally a letter arrived. The letter stated that I had been offered the job. I got the job! I got the job!! It was a conditional offer based on the performance I would exhibit in the training and then through the two-year probationary period. The training was about 30 days, 8 hours a day, 5 days a week. It required me to fully engage in all activities of the training sessions, to finish all the homework given daily, and to pass the exams at a certain percentage rate.

During the training it was impossible to maintain a full time or even part time job because of the demands and expectation that come with the TTC training process. It was understood at the beginning of training that the candidate must resign from his or her present employment in order to continue. As for me working at McDonald's, it wasn't a huge deal to give my boss two weeks' notice since I knew that, if I didn't pass the training, I could always go back.

Having to face the idea of leaving a current job must have been difficult for a husband or a wife or an individual who was the sole provider for his or her household. Imagine someone living from paycheque to paycheque, not knowing if they would pass the course. Of course, it was paid training but that didn't help after the training was over and you failed to make the cut. What would you do if you couldn't get your old job back? What about your kids? What about the bills that would pile up without having any income coming in regularly? Such thoughts and more course through the minds of the candidates but this is the journey that must be crossed in order to be a TTC operator.

In my training class, there was a gentleman who was a driving instructor, very knowledgeable about the rules on the road and personal driving. He was the first one to answer all the questions and to give input to all the other answers. He seemed to be the "head of the class." After realizing that the TTC expected candidates to resign from their current jobs, I could see that he was very troubled. One day, his seat was empty and I wondered what happened to him and why he stopped coming. It was made known that he didn't want to give up his job as a driving instructor. The month flew by and suddenly, despite the enormous amount of pressure upon all of us to pass, it was over. At home that evening after completing the full training, I told my mother what had happened. She said how proud she was of me and how great this opportunity was for me.

Since I had walked away from the basketball scholarship a few years back, there was a dimmer in my heart to live a passionate life. I thought I was a wandering soul in search of feeling significant and finding a sense of purpose. However, seeing that I was progressing with the TTC and accomplishing this goal, there was passion in my heart again. A passion to be the best TTC operator I could be, a passion to revitalize my life.

Things were finally turning around for me. I didn't know what lay ahead for me but I was determined to make an impact within this company. Up to this time there hadn't been a day go by that

Emma and I didn't spend time together. She shared in the joy and happiness of becoming a TTC operator. But what lay ahead would be such a shock to me. Never in my wildest dreams could I have anticipated that I would go through the types of experiences and trials that were waiting.

WALKING IN THE SHOES OF A TRANSIT OPERATOR III

Author: *How was your experience at the orientation, the first stage of becoming a TTC operator?*

Operator 1:   *I believe at my orientation (about seven years ago) I was extremely nervous because there were 500 other people seeking the same position that I wanted. I remember a representative standing up at the front of the room and beginning to talk. He spared no detail but told everyone the good, the bad and the ugly about the job. I could hear some people around me beginning to whisper when the spokesperson was talking about the ugly. I can honestly say that this job is not for everyone because not everyone is ready and willing to give up the time that they could devote to other areas of their lives, to work the hours we work or the schedules we do.*

Operator 2:   *When I went to the orientation there were a lot of people, old and young. It was very intimidating to say the least. It felt like my life was hanging in the balance, you know, but at the same time I was so excited to even be at the hotel. I remember there was a guy there who told us everything we needed to know about being an operator and he did not sugar coat anything. It was very informative and I made it through that stage and onto the interview. I passed the training regimen and have been working for eight months on the job now.*

Operator 3:   *I remember that day as if it was yesterday. On the morning of the orientation day I remember getting up feeling* extremely nervous because I knew that this was such a great opportunity and I didn't want to mess it up. My wife was very happy for me, my daughter was four years old at the time and so it felt as if the future of the family was on my shoulders. When I got there, there were 400 people pursuing the same position as I was. It has almost been seven years and I am still a TTC operator and not a day goes by that I do not thank this company for giving me this opportunity.

Operator 4:   It is pretty funny that you ask that because when I was sitting in the orientation meeting I knew exactly what I was getting into because I came from a trucking background. But after the meeting was done, I could hear people talking and saying that it wasn't for them because the hours and shifts were not conducive to the lifestyle that they were enjoying at present. I wonder how they are doing with their lives now. It has been over nine years and I wonder if they still have that lifestyle now as they did back then?

Operator 5:   When I got the letter to go to the orientation, I was the most excited individual on the planet. When the day came for me to attend, there was a long line up of other people who got the go ahead with the invitation to the hotel as well. There were a lot of people at the hotel, and all of us so eager to get just that driving position with the TTC. It was a little overwhelming to see such numbers.

Author: What was the most important thing that you got out of the job shadowing? Tell me about your experience.

Operator 6:   *I remember doing those assignments and realizing that being an operator was more than just driving around all day. I realized how much concentration is needed to operate the vehicle every second, every minute and every hour during the shift. I saw a cyclist jolting across the bus that I was on and the operator had to react quickly. I saw cars having no patience with the TTC vehicle, even though there were so many people onboard. I saw taxi cabs literally pull U-turns to pick up a customer and all of this happened in less than 20 minutes of being on the bus. It was a very interesting part of the recruitment process, that's for sure. Getting that first-hand experience beforehand from the operators themselves was invaluable.*

Operator 7:   *It was actually a beneficial assignment to perform job shadowing with the TTC because it allowed me to see and hear from the operators themselves about the job that I was pursuing. The majority of the concepts that I had surrounding this job previously were shattered. I must confess that a lot of them had a very negative outlook on the public and about other employees. Some operators gave me advice and told me to look for another occupation, while others told me how wonderful this job is. I guess the only way to formulate my own conclusion about this job was to try it out for myself—and I did!*

Operator 8:   *I gained an overall respect for the operators who literally serve the public for a living. During the process of my job shadowing interview, I witnessed a fight between two customers over the last empty seat left on the bus. I saw* *this and asked myself: "What other things has this bus driver observed throughout his career?"*

Operator 9:   *It was no easy task completing the job shadowing assignment, not because of the interviews but because I saw exactly what operators go through with the public, with the motorists and with all the other external factors on the road. So many details that are overlooked by the majority of the public. I saw just how hard it was for the operator to drive to the end destination.*

Operator 10:   *I had a chance to talk to a subway operator and it is a little different than being a bus operator. It is different in a sense that it is very isolated, a little separation from the public but similar with the bus operators because of the scheduling system. After hearing such scheduling and shifts from the operators themselves, it was quite clear that a lot of operators deal with the shifts that they get differently. My first thought after doing this assignment was if I really wanted to pursue this career.*

Author: *I know that the month long training to become an operator is tough. Tell me more about your experience, and how it affected your personal life?*

Operator 11:   *Well, it was very difficult to take in the fact that I had to quit my present job in order to participate in the training. However, I could understand why they had it set up like that. I think it's a good way to weed out flaky individuals, but it was literally a step of faith. If I didn't pass the tests, I would fail the training and then I would have no job to fall back on. I was truly happy for even being at this stage but it was heart wrenching to say the least.*

Operator 12: *The training was very difficult because I hadn't been at school for such a long time and I found the homework strenuous. I have three children at home so the idea of leaving my job was really unsettling. Questions went through my mind like: "What if I fail? What would happen to my kids?" My kids come first but ultimately the desire to get this job was more than my fear because accomplishing this training would bring my family better security.*

Operator 13: *It was so long ago but I remember that the training class is like 30 days or something like that. But we had eight or nine people in the class and it was not easy. The TTC does a great job with its instructors and weeding out people. At the end of the training only three of us passed and it was not because of lack of instruction. It's just not for everyone. I am glad I gave my all and got in. I am still grateful for this job and it has been over nine years now.*

Operator 14: *I remember the morning of the critical driving test, I was really nervous. If I failed this test, I would go home and have to look for another job since I had left my job because of the training. I could see that there were a lot of people in my class that were visibly shaken. It was now or never. However the instructors did an amazing job calming our nerves. I gave it my all and I passed. I am grateful for this job because it was definitely a long road to travel and a difficult path to walk down to get to where I am now.*

Operator 15: *I have heard so many people say that being a bus driver is so easy. But if they only knew the sacrifices that were made at the start of the process, I believe their perspectives would change.*

Be kind, don't judge, and have respect for others.
If we can all do this, the world would be a better place.
The point is to teach this to the next generation.

—Jasmine Guinness

CHAPTER 3

IS THIS JOB
REALLY FOR ME?

I remember at my orientation the TTC spokesman had talked about the life of an operator and how different it was in comparison to jobs with normal working hours. The TTC frontline work was mainly based on seniority and shift work. He made it clear to everyone in the room on that morning that operator schedules would be tough on certain groups of people and, in order to be successful away from work and in your personal life, you would need to have a lot of understanding from the people close to you. There would be family events, weddings, parties or special occasions that would have to be missed due to the shift work scheduling. At the end of my training regimen, the idea of my life changing so much due to the working schedule really didn't sink in since I thought that it wouldn't be as difficult as what the TTC spokesman said. When it was time to be assigned to a home bus division, I was told I would be posted at a division in the west end of Toronto.

A few other new operators from my class were also placed at the same division and I was glad that I wouldn't be alone in a new place. The TTC gave us a date on which we would meet the management team of our home division and get to know the layout. I was given a booklet, a welcome package, from the division. In it were the bus routes and the directions needed to navigate through them. There was just one thing wrong with the welcome package: I was terrible with directions! I had no idea how to determine north, south, east or west and that was how the TTC described the directions for each route.

Throughout the bus division tour other operators were on their breaks or getting ready to start their shift. As we did our tour around the division many operators would talk to us about our experience so far. Since we haven't done any official driving as TTC employees, the experienced operators flooded us with advice on how to treat this job and what to expect. They offered their help and guidance if we ever needed it with regards to the navigation of the routes, or trying to locate where different things were placed around the division and even how to deal with the public.

However, the common theme and conversation amongst the majority of operators that we talked to was the fact that there would be a high possibility of losing friends and even relationships due to the shifts of the job. But I paid no attention to such doom and gloom talk because I believed that the connection that Emma and I had would be strong enough to overcome anything. I was sent home that evening after completing all the necessary courses of action and seeing from the divisional point of view how things operated. I had met my boss and the management team and I had been given my first shift as a TTC operator for the following day.

That night I opened up to Emma about my fears in relation to my inability to follow directions and navigating the bus routes. We looked over the welcome package together and, with her comforting words, she made me feel that everything would work out for the better. The first night I was being dropped off at work by Emma and knowing that we would not be spending that evening together made me feel sad. Even though I was deeply humbled to get this job and I accepted all the sacrifices that I had made in order to achieve this opportunity, that first night away from Emma gave me a reality check.

I was now a career man, with responsibilities, and looking into her eyes as I shut the car door and headed towards the entrance of my division was very difficult. When I went through my first few shifts as an operator, I realized these shifts were the exact opposite of Emma's working hours. During those beginning shifts of my career I didn't see her as much as I had before. I started wondering to myself if this the life of a TTC operator. As time went by my heart grew heavier and heavier knowing that having such a job based on shift work would dramatically change my life and mainly my relationship life with Emma.

The job itself was amazing. Working with the public, working with other like minded operators and being a young man with a great paying job, I truly felt alive. However, as time went by, I saw how truly vulnerable TTC operators including myself really are to the public. I saw in a very short time the ugliness of people more than I saw their beauty. As stated before, at the beginning of my career I was struggling navigating most of the routes at that particular division. But I sought out advice about the routes from various sources such as other operators and supervisors.

After being reassured with the answers, I would drive the route in my own vehicle with Emma and we would try to identify landmarks so that it would be easier for me to pinpoint where I should or should not turn. But there was still that nervousness in my stomach every time I would start my shift because, instead of doing it in my own personal vehicle, it was with eager passengers anxious to get to where they needed to go. I remember on one particular shift how nervous I was since the area that I was driving was totally unknown to me. The shift was an overnight shift, making it even worse. The night was so dark that I was concerned whether the landmarks that I had marked would be visible.

Having my welcome package and the personal notes that Emma and I had made gave me hope that I would get through the shift without any directional problems. As I was waiting on the platform for my bus, I anxiously flipped through the welcome package and my notes just trying to get the last minute preparation in my brain. By the time the bus came, the platform was already full of people waiting to get on. The operator and I exchanged pleasantries and he wished me all the best. I got in the driver's seat and organized myself. By the time I was ready to move, the bus had a full standing load. I took a deep breath and off I went to start my new bus driving career.

At the beginning, I was doing very well. It was a straight road with no concerns about having to make a left or right turn. But then I came to an intersection that got me stumped. I didn't know whether I was supposed to make a turn or proceed through the intersection. It was really dark and I couldn't make out the street name. At the same time, I was so certain that this was where I was supposed to turn. I tried frantically to look over my welcome pack, the route description and even the notes that I had made. The bus didn't move for almost five minutes but it seemed like forever. As the five-minute mark rolled around and as several traffic lights cycled through, I began to hear mumbling and complaining from the passengers, whispers as to why the bus wasn't moving. A voice that called out from the back: "Driver! Move the bus!" And another voice saying: "Come on driver! I'm late!"

By this time, I was sitting in that driver seat with sweat forming on the top of my brow. Even though I had the personal aids with me, the pressure that I felt was so overwhelming that I totally had a brain freeze. There was an assistance on the TTC vehicle itself for me to use in the form of a trump unit, a two-way communication system between driver and supervisor. Despite having this tool to help me get through this situation, the commotion rising on the bus echoed through me. A passenger was making their way to the front of the bus, asking other passengers to let her pass. I thought that I was probably about to encounter my first complaint and I braced myself for this. I felt a tap on my shoulder, but I didn't turn around at first, feeling ashamed for my lack of action. Another tap. I knew that I would have to engage with her now because she wasn't going away.

As I wiped the sweat from my eyes, I turned to see a small woman looking back at me with a big smile. She motioned for me to bend my head towards her so that she could talk to me. She knew that I was confused and didn't know if I should turn the bus or go straight. She sensed that I was a new operator because I didn't even have the TTC uniform on yet. Amongst all the negative comments that were coming my way, this little lady said the sweetest thing to me. All she said was: "I will help you." I thanked her from the bottom of my heart for the kindness and her willingness to help me get through what I thought was the end of the world for me. She stood at the front of the bus right beside me and gave me instructions on where to go and where to turn.

That lady's kindness had such a great impact on me early on in my career that I remembered her two years later when she was my passenger again on another bus route. She didn't recognize me, but I recognized her and I told her what she had done for me two years before. To this day, if ever saw her on the streets I would immediately recognize her and it has been more than seven years. The beauty of a simple act can go a long way in someone's life. Passengers can truly make a difference on how an operator feels, whether for good or bad.

That was one experience I will not forget but I also remember one that almost caused me to resign from my job within not even one month of starting. I was given a last-minute overnight shift as I was waiting at my division to be detailed work. So I couldn't really prepare for my shift by understanding the route and turns because I was on "open report" (to be explained later). After being detailed work for that overnight shift, I had little time to get to the location where I would start my shift. I quickly gathered my belongings and welcome package and off I went. On this particular route, at a certain time it would turn into an overnight bus and continue on a different route pattern.

The first part of the route was pretty much straightforward and I got a handle on it very easily. But then the time came when I was supposed to switch to the overnight route. The area was unknown to me and, at every bus stop or traffic stop, I quickly opened up the welcome package to see how to do this overnight route. I got really confused and flustered. I had flashbacks of the previous experience when I didn't know which way to go. I turned around to see if I could ask for help but there was only one passenger onboard and was fast asleep at the back of the bus. I thought to myself that, if I had made a wrong turn, it wouldn't be that bad because at least there was only one passenger instead of a packed bus.

I checked the welcome package and concluded I needed to turn the bus. As I did so there wasn't any indication from that man at the back of the bus that I was going the wrong way. I continued to drive this unknown street. I no longer saw any bus stops on either side, and the stop announcement that called out the stops didn't call out anymore stops. Suddenly the silence on the bus was broken by the voice of the solo male passenger: "Driver! Where the fuck are you going? Where the fuck are we? Are you a fucking idiot?"

I stopped the bus and looked back at him. I confessed that I was a new operator and that I didn't know the area very well. I apologized and told him that I would call my supervisor and ask for directions. He exploded on me and continued to swear at me using all sorts of language. Charging to the front of the bus, he yelled at me right at my face and told me to open up the front door to let him out. So I did. I sat on the bus alone feeling like a piece of dirt, lower than dirt. I had never been yelled at like that before. I only had a few weeks on the job and felt humiliated beyond words. I bent my head over the steering wheel while thoughts that maybe this job wasn't right for me filled my mind. Could I handle being yelled at like that and treated with such disrespect for the rest of my TTC career? Should I resign right now and save myself from other situations like this in the future?

As I was contemplating quitting, the supervisor in charge for the overnight shifts in the office returned my call on the radio. I apologized for going off route and I told her that I wanted to quit. I was humiliated, not because I went off route, but because the words of that man left such an awful taste in my mouth. I felt so low hearing such words aimed at me and I really didn't want to be a TTC operator anymore. After venting my sadness and resentment to the supervisor, the tenderness of her voice and words soothed my heart. She told me not to quit and that everything would be OK. She said she believed in me and that, if I could stick this out, then things would get better. Her mother-like tenderness lifted my heart and she helped me get back on the route and told me that everything would be fine. The dark cloud started to lift and I began to feel at ease enough to continue on with the shift and complete it.

Operators deal with thousands of different personalities and temperaments on a daily basis. You can just imagine the number verbal comments operators receive when things go wrong for the passengers. I began to see that being an operator was like having a target on your back against which certain people could express their anger and frustration. I talked with senior operators and friends just starting out to see if I wasn't the only one who had such unruly passengers. The results shocked me a little. The majority of my friends and other veteran operators had either been verbally looked down upon or felt humiliated by the actions of some passengers.

I was shocked because I thought that being a TTC operator was all about service to the public and the public would at least appreciate what we, operators, do for them. I thought that the hours that we work, the time and energy that we give to the public would be looked upon by them as an admirable thing. However, it was starting to appear that it wasn't. I knew that millions of passengers rode the TTC, and that it was impossible to please everyone all the time. What I didn't know at the time was that, because the workers at the frontline are constantly in the eyes of the public, it is the transit operators who bear the brunt of abuse.

However, I also heard stories and shared stories of my own about passengers who offered a helping hand, or that spoke words of gratitude and appreciation for the safe ride. The idea of giving up on this job or throwing in the towel began to fade when I saw that the majority of the passengers were in fact respectful and civilized. I saw that I wasn't alone and that other operators and supervisors had gone through what I experienced. I could take refuge knowing that they hadn't quit. The first few months were very difficult and the adjustment was slow. I was getting the scraps for my working schedule, usually overnights and my off days weren't really allowing me to spend time with Emma. Despite that I was enjoying being a TTC operator and making new friends within the company.

WALKING IN THE SHOES OF A TRANSIT OPERATOR IV

Author: *How was your experience as a TTC operator during the first few months on the job?*

Operator 1: *If there is a person who said that when he or she first started that he or she wasn't at all nervous I would say that is impossible. It is a nerve wracking experience because you feel as if the world is on your shoulders. You think that any mistake could cost you your job, but that is not normally the case.*

Operator 2: *The first shift on my own, without my divisional trainer, of course I was nervous. I was driving the TTC vehicle extremely slow because I didn't want to get in any accident or even miss a stop. But over time the level of confidence starts to build.*

Operator 3: *The first month on the job was a great experience because I received so much help from the management and the operators. My division was like a big family and everyone was looking out for each other. Regarding the public, I didn't really have any trouble with them, and they didn't have any trouble with me!*

Operator 4: *It was a tough transition from working a job that required me to deal with customers over the phone to now dealing with them face to face. What I mean by face to face is that, even though I tried to please everyone, I really can't and I get to see their reaction first hand. It was an eye opener for sure to see the things that TTC operators* *really go through when I was doing my job shadowing but now even more so as I experienced it first hand.*

Operator 5: *I know at the orientation the spokesperson talked about that. I really didn't pay no attention to it because I thought he was over-exaggerating, but going through the few months on the job, he was totally right. I started to miss out on certain events with family and friends and my schedule was all over the place. I didn't have a set schedule yet and it was really taking a toll on my life at the time and I just had shy of a month. I even contemplated resigning but had second thoughts because other senior operators said that it would get better over the years.*

Operator 6: *During my first month I really wasn't given any overnight shifts because of the little seniority that I did have. I had lots of split shifts and, having a family at home, working those split shifts really hampered my time with my son. But I knew that the reason for me pursuing the job was because of a better life for my family. I also knew that the beginning stages as a TTC operator would be difficult but over the years once more new individual join the TTC team I would get a better working selection. But I would say it took over two years to be able to work decent shifts.*

Author: *How were your encounters with the public at the beginning of your career?*

Operator 7: *I remember the first couple of weeks being new on the job, which was over nine years ago. Because I was doing the overnight shifts, I saw more fights than I had ever seen* *before. Overnight is a totally different environment and passengers than the day time passengers. Especially on Friday and Saturday nights, I would say that 90% of the passengers that I picked up on the overnight route were drunk.*

Operator 8: *Being an operator during those times really opened my eyes to the world of people uncensored. I had a few passengers yell at me for driving too slow and it was because I was just trying to get familiar with the route. I think it was very difficult to realize that.*

Operator 9: *My first day on the job, I was so excited to get out on my own and serve the public. What I mean by that was that before I was an official employee for the TTC, I had to drink with an instructor who would correct me and guide me on what to do while I was driving. My first day on the job, however, I was doing an overnight route and picked up a bunch of guys who were apparently drunk. As they got onboard, waves of criticism about me being an operator came out of their mouths. I guess because they thought I was picking up too many people from the stops that they began to throw cuss words at me. I felt totally embarrassed and humiliated with the comments that were being said because everyone on the bus heard what they said. But I have learned to shut my ears and let negative words roll off my back from negative passengers. I have been working for the TTC commission for over 15 years now, so having the ability to pick your battles is crucial in keeping sane on this job.*

Operator 10: *What the public needs to understand is that their words truly do affect an operator and even though we really try* *not to let one unruly passenger ruin our day, it sometimes does happen. My first encounter with an unruly customer was when there was a detour on the route and, even though I announced it over the PA a few times, the man got upset and said that he didn't know. It was apparent that he had his headphones on and, because of that, he didn't hear the announcement. However, being verily new the words of that man really hit me because I was doing everything by the book. It took a while to realized that working with the public, particularly the amount of passengers that we operators deal with, you need to have thick skin.*

Operator 11: *Being a new kid on the block, learning new skills, learning to make new friends in a new environment could be very stressful. Good thing I came out of a customer service background and it was very easy to provide such service to the passengers. I had a great time at the beginning of my career because I really enjoy being in the presence of people. I am a single individual so the schedules and shifts didn't really affect my personal life because I just reorganized my life schedule to fit my personal life. However, I could see how being married and having a family at the beginning of the TTC career could definitely be difficult.*

Operator 12: *I had some great experiences when I was going through my first few months on the job. I had so many people offering their help to me and even appreciated the fact that I got them to their destination safe and sound. It has been three years now working for TTC and every day I have counted my blessings because I have not had any bad experiences with the public so far.*

What people who are doing shift work
or managing shift workers or deciding
to put people on shift schedules to begin with
should realize that we're not robots.
—Jessa Gamble

CHAPTER 4

SHIFTS

A TTC frontline worker's schedule is based on seniority as previous mentioned. Basically the more years you've worked, the more and better selection of work you can choose from. The schedule for an operator changes every six weeks (and sometimes more frequently than that depending on certain holidays and events that occur throughout the year). During the half way marker of the six-week period, operators have a chance to choose their work for the following 'board' (every six-week working schedule is called a 'board'). So the most senior operator would get the opportunity to look over the next board and all the shifts that are available to all operators at that division. When the selection time came for the veteran operators to choose the work for the new board, such selection periods would last several days until all the operators, from the most senior to the most junior had completed the process.

I never had done shift work before and this whole selection process was new and strange to me. At first, by the time my name was called to choose my shift for the following six weeks, there was hardly anything left: no weekends off, no regular hours to select. Often the only shifts that were left for me were for overnight work, with Tuesday / Wednesday off. It was a huge adjustment to say the least. Each time the selection process took place, it made me realize just how important seniority is to the TTC operators. Since I didn't have much seniority at the time, the shifts that I was getting were the scraps at the bottom of the barrel. The leftovers. It was very difficult to come from a job that has regular hours into a career that is all about seniority.

There was another problem for me personally that was already starting to emerge at the beginning of my career. It was a problem that I would face throughout my career, a problem that operators before me had faced and operators after me would continue to face. Shift work for me personally was the hardest thing to adjust to and accept, because I felt like it literally took up my whole day, without leaving any time for enjoyment and leisure. Of course there are some operators who would say that having shift work gave them even more of an opportunity to increase their leisure time and get errands done at times of the day when other people were working. However, it was the same shifts that caused many struggles in my personal life.

In order for you to try to walk in the shoes of the operator, and understand how such shifts affect their personal lives, here are the shift options that a TTC operator has to choose from:

Split shift

A split shift is essentially when an operator would work a scheduled eight-hour shift but would have a schedule break in the middle of the shift. For example, if an operator is scheduled to work from 6:00 am until 6:00 pm, he/she would work from 6:00 am until 10:00

am, which would be the first part of the shift. From 10:00 am until 2:00 pm the operator would take a break. He/she would then be free to do whatever they would like within this four-hour break. At 2:00 pm the operator would return to work and complete the shift from 2:00 pm until 6:00 pm. As you can see it is a very long day for the operator.

There are other versions of the split shift with different start times and longer and shorter breaks in the middle. Some operators use the break in between the working shift to do errands or go to the local gym. Others go home to rest. When I first started working these type of shifts, I was designated to an area which was at the other end of the city and it wasn't logical to travel back home in the break time. So often times I would use the time of my break to sleep in my car and recuperate. It wasn't unusual at my home division to see cars lined up in the parking lot with TTC operators sleeping in them.

Each operator has his or her opinion on working the split shift, for me personally it was extremely tough trying to balance work and life. As I didn't live close to the division, the average time I would be away from home due to work and travel time would be 13-15 hours a day. Many days coming home from work I was totally exhausted mentally from the long stretched-out day and the affects of travelling back home from facing the public for more than nine hours. Many times when I got home all I wanted to do was crash out. This started to affect my time spent with Emma and began to eat away at the close intimacy we had shared. She would get upset, telling me that I no longer arranged date nights or that I didn't want to do anything together. The reality was that I was running on an empty energy tank. All I wanted after work was to go to bed and sleep because in just a little while longer I would have to get up and do it all over again. During the early years of my TTC career, it was tough. But I can say now that those difficult times were actually building my mental toughness and training me for things to come.

Regulars

A "regular" is a shift that usually gets taken by more senior operators because of its absence of split shifts. It's basically the shift that most resembles a normal working day. It doesn't have a break in between like the split shift, but it does have a break that can last anywhere from 10 minutes to 30 minutes. The breaks are usually called "step backs" in these circumstances. For example, an operator can pick a regular shift that might start at 5:00 am and finish at 1:00 pm. There would be a 15-30 minute break, most likely at 10:30 am. Of course working times do vary for each operator based on what the operator chooses in the selection date but this is essentially what the "regular" shift is.

Open report

Open report is a shift that has spare drivers waiting at the division in case another operator calls in sick at late notice or an operator takes an emergency leave for whatever reason. Having a spare driver is crucial due to the fact that the work from that absent operator needs to be filled or it gets cancelled affecting the passengers who rely on that particular vehicle for that particular time. One of the spare operators on "open report" can then fill that post. This type of shift is very common in bus transit companies throughout the world not just within the TTC community.

There were times when I was on "open report" and, at the beginning of my career, this time made for some very anxious moments. When you are on "open report," you really don't know what type of work you will be getting until an operator has booked off. So when I was new I dreaded being on "open report" because I didn't know beforehand what shift I was going to get and I didn't want to be unprepared. When my name was called I would frankly ask other operators for help and advice. Thankfully, all of them offered their help without any hesitation.

Vacation board

The vacation board is a type of work that is available on the selection board during the selection process that basically allows operators' work to be covered by another operator when one is on vacation. Whatever their shifts would have been, this work becomes available for other operators to cover. Many operators love the idea of choosing work on vacation board because it gives variety and mixes up the work schedule for them, getting out of the mundane of doing the same work for six weeks.

Spareboard

Spareboard is another shift that can be chosen when it is the operator's turn to choose his or her shift during the selection day. When spareboard is selected, it means that the shift for the following day is not known to the operator until 5:00 pm on the day before.

For example, if an operator is on spareboard, he or she will not know what type of work, what route he or she is doing, what time he or she is starting or finishing until 5:00 pm the day before the shift actually starts. So if I wanted to know what I am doing tomorrow I would have to wait to call in and request what my schedule is after 5:00 pm today. Again there are operators who love the variety that this can bring.

This type of shift allocation was very hard for me to deal with because it was difficult for me to plan things with Emma. She would ask me if I wanted to get together for a date or if I was available to attend a family function. But I wouldn't know what my shift was for the following day until 5:00 pm. So most times I would tell her that I would have to get back to her. This particular shift also had a negative effect on Emma, my friends and family. I would miss a lot of events when I got spareboard for my working schedule.

Compressed

The "compressed" shift is one of the shifts that appeals to an operator who loves having an extra day off. So, rather than the normal two days off, it would be three.

At the same time, it is one of the longest shifts that the TTC offers. An operator could have a work day of 10 hours of actual driving or work time with a break in between. The break usually is not as long as one in a "split shift" and not as short as a "regular" shift. So an operator could work from 6:00 am to 11:00 am with a one-hour break, and then return to work from 12:00 pm until 5:00 pm. It is a very mentally draining day, if you imagine being in the driving seat for 10 plus hours in a day (and again the start times and break times can vary). So, with the longer hours, compressed work comes with an additional day off, but the day off varies within the week.

Special

There is a called "special" shift which allows the operator to work less than eight hours, but get paid for eight hours and it usually comes with weekends off. Usually this type of work is taken by senior operators who have paid their dues over the years working split shifts and overnight shifts. There is something called a "two-piece special" which has the same concept, but has a break in between in order to extend the shift time to revolve around the morning rush hour and evening rush hour (as if it was a split shift).

For example an operator would come to work for 9:00 am until 12:00 pm and have a break from 12:00 pm until 1:00 pm. Then the operator would return to work from 1:00 pm until 4:00 pm. So you can see that the operator worked less than eight hours but got paid for eight hours.

These are the majority of the shifts that are available to the operators. The timings and situations might change but the principles remain the same. There are also overnight shifts, but these do not have breaks or splits. The operator would drive all night without any break. This was the shift that I preferred when I'd had a few years on the job because I hated the fact of having to be in my work clothes for more than eight hours a day. I would do overnight because it was straight eight hours and then I could go home.

If you really understand the shifts that are offered to the TTC operators, you can clearly see the personal sacrifice each operator undertakes. I am convinced that not everyone can successfully be a TTC operator because it is not as easy as some people might think.

In my first few years on the job, I experienced some of the most difficult times in my life so far. The shifts that were left when it came to my turn to choose didn't really leave me with any good options. Board after board I felt as if I could never get a decent work pattern established in order to spend more time with my family, friends and Emma. Shift work is extremely difficult not only on the individual but everyone within that individual's life. It's no secret that working shift takes up a large chunk of time and personal rejuvenation which ultimately means the lack of time with love ones and other things.

In order to have a successful balance, life as a shift worker requires having an understanding family and friends. The people around you need to understand and realize that shift work is not an ordinary job because the hours are not like any ordinary job. It literally does take a toll on one's body and especially mentally. Often times I've heard people say: "All TTC operators do is sit and drive, it can't be that hard." Little do they realize that dealing with hundreds of people every single day for long periods is very taxing on the mind. More often than not, I was totally exhausted mentally by the time I finished my shifts. It is crucial to have your close ones realize and understand this. Since there will be times when all you want to do after working such shifts is rest, to have people around you that don't understand that will most definitely be detrimental to any relationship.

There is another aspect that is often overlooked: the loneliness endured on the job. Despite being in the midst of hundreds of people on an hourly basis, it is a very lonely job. With social media now and the increase in patrons who like to record everything that they see during their day, operators can easily feel as if the public is against them. There are operators who go into the washroom to have a bite to eat for fear of being posted on YouTube for "eating on the job" or for fear of complaints reaching their supervisor. There are many operators who change their clothes immediately when they finish their shift in order to avoid scrutiny from the public.

I remember a few years ago, there was a public outcry around an operator who got a coffee in the middle of the night, and an operator who used the washroom in the middle of a route. I read a comment on YouTube that bus drivers should have a way to use the washroom while they sat driving, so that the need of using the washroom didn't disrupt the service time. This is the type of mentality that's out there! The newspapers often report incidents about TTC operators doing things wrong, and this perspective of wrongdoing spreads all over the city. Because one operator acted this way, people assume that all operators act this way. It is totally unfair to paint all operators with the same brush but that is what usually happens when something goes wrong with the TTC.

At the beginning of my career I was a fun filled individual, constantly enjoying the presence of people around me and always expressing my joy with laughter. But being secluded from people for several hours a day, and being exposed to such intense surveillance from the public brought my spirit down. It was apparent that I was changing and changing for the worst. Little by little my walls went up against the public. Feeling such pressure from the public, I would often choose overnight shifts whenever I could, just to lessen the opportunity for scrutiny. But even during the night, the only company I had was my own.

Being an operator is not a job for just anyone. In my opinion it's for those who can endure the shifts, the loneliness and the scrutiny and still have a tough mental focus. An operator experiences a lot more than people realize, and the majority of these things are dealt with at a mental and emotional level.

WALKING IN THE SHOES OF A TRANSIT OPERATOR V

Author: *How has the shift work and schedule affected your personal life and life in general?*

Operator 1:   *The split shift is one of those things that you just have to deal with. You need to have an understanding wife and family. It does take up your whole day though, and when I am home it takes great effort to stay up with my kids and play with them. Usually I am awake for 17 hours a day with just work and family life. Thankfully I have an understanding wife.*

Operator 2:   *Split shifts were definitely a challenge to say the least, because of making the necessary adjustments in my life. I came from a 9-5 job in the business world, with weekends off and evenings spent with my kids. The split shift was a wakeup call to the realities of life as an operator. It was just what the TTC spokesman had said at the orientation, that shift work is definitely not like other regular working jobs. The spokesman was right and it was very hard to adjust my lifestyle around my work.*

Operator 3:   *I have seven years on the job. I'm married and have two teenage children and I was very humbled by the opportunity that the TTC gave me. At the start of my career it was extremely hard to balance work and time with family and friends. I remember a veteran operator told me that I would lose friends because of the shifts. At the time I didn't believe him, but looking back on it, he was exactly right. I can only decline my friends' invitations for so long before they stop asking, and that's what happened.*

Operator 4: *Three years on as an operator, and I know that the split shift can be very stressful to the people close to you because it affects them as well. I have to confess though that I love having split shifts and the ability to pick my own off days. I live close to my division and I get to do a lot of stuff during my shifts that I wouldn't normally do if I worked a regular working day. Plus, I organize my life with my wife so we don't need to hire a babysitter to watch our child. It works for me, but I appreciate that I am one of the few that this shift works out for.*

Operator 5: *Of course having a straight eight-hour shift is ideal, but I try to make the best of having split shifts. I try and go to the gym and workout in between work shifts. I have lost a lot of weight because of the time that I have during these breaks.*

Operator 6: *Well I have 28 years of service with the TTC and I must say that all the years have been wonderful. At the beginning of my career it was definitely hard because usually you get a work pattern that does not correspond with the days off that your family and friends have. But eventually it does get better. I have been doing "regulars" for many years now so basically 4 am-12:30 pm. Yes, yes I know I have to wake up around 2 am every day, but I am used to it.*

Operator 7: *I have over 30 years with the TTC and yes the worst thing about the job is the split shifts, but it does get better over the years. I remember losing lots of friends because our job is not a regular 8 to 4 job. But that is the nature of* the beast when you first join. It is a great job but the shifts are really crappy at the start of the career. However, after 30 years, I can pick the shifts that work for me and my family. I hardly have any close friends outside of the company now. I guess the operators coming into the company have to pay their dues but it does get better, they just need to hang in there.

Operator 8:   For the first four years I was stuck working the overnight bus on the Bloor / Danforth with Tuesdays and Wednesdays off. So it was hard to maintain a social life but, after 25 years I guess I paid my dues. It is tough at the beginning, not a lot of people can handle it.

Operator 9:   It's been more than four years now and it has been a bumpy ride so far with the shifts and days off. But I was brought up with a set of values to cherish and to be thankful for what you have. Getting this job with the TTC has been good for me. There are not a lot of jobs out there that offer what the TTC does.

Operator 10:   I tell the younger operators that they have got to put in their time with the company. I have worked the overnight shifts, the split shifts and had my days off during the week. So after 25 years, it has been wonderful to get off at around 12:30 pm and have the whole day to myself or to be with my family.

Operator 11:   I have worked for more than 20 years. The TTC has been good to me and I am working great shifts now. At the beginning it is very tough, but it does get better with time.

Operator 12:   *This is a great company to work for. Operators have the ability to organize their lives and choose the shifts that cater to their needs and the needs of their family. There are many operators like me who are able to re-arrange their schedule to fit their home lifestyle.*

Operator 13:   *It is great that TTC offers schedules that change every six weeks. I can choose day work, evening work or night work. Those huge splits are sometimes brutal but it is necessary because of the rush hour demands. It is definitely hard to live a normal life and have a proper routine during the first couple of years on the job.*

Operator 14:   *Honestly, being an operator can sometimes be very lonely, even though you are surrounded by so many people, you feel alone a lot of the time. It is lonely because we spend more time on the bus than we do with our own friends and family.*

Operator 15:   *I have been working as a subway operator for quite some time now and I absolutely love my job. Of course being in the tunnel can be lonely sometimes but it is what it is.*

Operator 16:   *Of course it can be lonely at times but I try to interact with my passengers as much as possible and make it a fun experience. You have to have a little fun on this job otherwise you will have an emotional meltdown!*

When things are bad, we take comfort
in the thought that they could always get worse.
And when they are, we find hope in the thought
that things are so bad they have to get better.
—Malcolm s. Forbes

CHAPTER 5

―――――――

RISE AND FALL

As the months went by I started to have a little more seniority which meant I was able to choose better work than previously. TTC was hiring more operators and that was always a good sign for me because then it would increase my seniority. Throughout the many shifts that were allocated to me and the ones that were left for me to choose from, Emma was right by my side. For the many commutes to and from work, it was Emma who allowed me to borrow her car. Often, when she needed the car, she would drive me to work and go home and then pick me up again, taking several hours out of her day.

We had officially been in a relationship for quite some time and, seeing all the sacrifices that she made for me, I had fallen more in love with her. A new bus division was about to open up and many operators were forced to make the switch from the previous division to the new one. I was one of the operators chosen to go and, though it was closer to Scarborough where I lived at the time, it was still in the west end of Toronto, quite a distance from my home. Emma didn't complain at all about the distance driving to and from work to pick me up. It was so reassuring having her by my side. During my career up to this point, I was enthralled by her love and acts of kindness. I had known for a long time that Emma was the right woman for me and that the time to put a ring on her finger was near.

The night I proposed to her was magical to say the least. I had a lot of help from her family and friends because I wanted it to be very special. I arranged a limousine to pick her up and to take us to a restaurant. As we were out enjoying each other's company, back at her house all of her close friends and family were setting up a little gathering for when she got back home. At the restaurant I had arranged for the live band, with the help of the manager, to allow me the opportunity to have access to one of their microphones so that I could say something to her.

The restaurant was full of people, but when I got up to the microphone it felt as if it was just the two of us. I asked Emma to accompany me and I opened my heart to her. When I got down on one knee and asked her to marry me and she said yes, I was the happiest man on earth. On the way back, the limousine dropped her off at her place and I told her that I was going home and would call her later. Little did she know that there was a group of people waiting for her, to share with her how much she meant to them all.

After walking in, she was asked to sit in the middle of a circle surrounded by all her loved ones. One by one they took turns expressing to Emma how much they loved her and how much she meant to them. As that was happening, I was at my place trying to make it as romantic as possible for the two of us. There were candles and flower petals everywhere. When the meeting at her place was over, I sent her a message asking her to come over and meet me at my place. My queen was on her way and I was putting everything in order, just the way I wanted it to be. She entered the house and I led her to the room and asked her to sit down. I shared with her how I felt about her and how I vowed to grow old with her.

I was 23 at the time. Newly engaged and newly employed, things were looking up. The thought of missing such a great basketball opportunity and failing to accomplish my childhood dream no longer entered my head. I had a bright outlook in life, a positive attitude towards people and such a passion for wanting to be the best that I could be in every area of my life.

However, staying positive wasn't always easy, especially having to deal with the public on such a large scale. I always wanted to go the extra mile and go out of my way to help. But when I started to see the ugly side of people my attitude changed. I remember one incident when the bus in front of me was out of service due to a mechanical issue. People getting on my bus gave me dirty looks as if I was late, when the situation had nothing to do with me. One time I was driving a route where the bus service wasn't as frequent as on other routes. There was a 10-minute "headway," so the amount of time a passenger waits standing at a bus stop should be no more than 10 minutes. It was a very cold morning and, since the buses were idling throughout the night, when the morning shift came, there were a lot of buses that were covered in frost.

That morning I saw operators scraping frost from the mirrors with plastic scrapers and revving the bus engines to try to get some heat generated inside. It was so cold and many mechanical troubles ravaged those old GM buses. As I was driving to start my shift, I saw that the bus that was supposed to be 10 minutes in front of me was broken down and "out of service." So I knew that the people who were waiting for that bus would now be waiting for my bus. Instead of waiting 10 minutes for a bus, the customers would have been waiting 20 minutes in the freezing cold by the time I arrived.

Getting to the first stop of the route, I saw nothing but angry faces and lips that were so tight with frustration and ready to explode. I opened the door and as expected I heard nothing but negativity and comments about how bad an operator I was. I heard passengers say that they were going to report me to my boss. Others didn't comment verbally but I could feel their bad attitude towards me and that just brought my spirit down. Bus stop after bus stop I heard the same things about how late I was and that I made them late for work. They had no idea that the bus ahead of me was out of service and that I was right on schedule.

I kept my mouth closed because I realized that the public really doesn't want to know the reasons why they were waiting for an extended period. They just wanted to vent their frustration and I was the one who was going to get it on this particular day. What if they knew that the bus in front of me was supposed to be there but because of the natural elements it was unsafe to drive that TTC vehicle? What if the public knew exactly what had happened? Would the complaints stop and would there be more of an understanding rather than this disapproval? I don't think so. In many similar situations I had given out such information in order to try to ease the passengers' frustration. But there were still many who wouldn't care about the explanation and would keep on with their negative attacks and insults.

The humiliation that I felt that day, despite the fact that the situation was completely out of my control, was so damaging. I can totally understand the frustrations that the public has but what they need to come to grips with is that there are situations that happen on the transit system that are not the direct fault of the operator. Now, think about the many TTC operators who have gone through the same situations and have encountered similar attacks. It is a day-to-day occurrence. The TTC receives many complaints from the public that have no real foundation when they are investigated.

There are so many advertising campaigns against bullying in the schools, in the cyber world and in the workplace. But what about TTC operators and how they too could be subjected to bullying? The definition of a "bully" is a person who uses strength or power to harm or intimidate those who are weaker, or the use of superior strength or influence to intimidate, typically to force him or her to do what one wants. I am in no way saying that TTC operators are weaker or stronger but that, because their professionalism and code of conduct, it appears that they are weaker. When I was driving the bus and when things happened that were out of my control and a few of the passengers would get unruly, I would have to absorb the insults without retaliating.

Stop bullying campaigns have been very popular in recent years and rightly so, for without the awareness and a non-acceptance stance being taken, there would be no change. However, I would go as far as to add to that a "stop bullying transit operators" campaign, because there were days when I felt as if I were being bullied by every passenger that came onto my bus. Many times when there was a subway closure or an accident and the bus that I was driving had to detour or some other incident adding more time to the passengers, usually I would get a lot of stares or rude comments.

I'm not saying that every experience that I had with the public was a negative one. I encountered a lot of amazing passengers. Many dentist appointments were needed because of the candies I received from elderly ladies on the bus. However, it was the negative experiences that really had more impact on me. I guess it was because of the feeling of not being treated as an equal, as a human being.

Such struggles at work was compounded by the struggles mentally I was facing as my marriage day approached. I found myself questioning my ability in being a husband. What did a "good hus-band" even look like? Was I mature enough to handle the respon-sibilities of being a husband? Or was I too young to make such a huge commitment? So many thoughts raced through my mind about being a young married man. And I kept them to myself as I felt embarrassed to even share them with anyone.

But what I did know was that this woman had been there for me when I had nothing and was working at a minimum wage job. She had been there when I had no idea of what I wanted to do with my life and had no real goal to pursue. She had been there when I applied for the TTC, throughout the job shadowing process and the training process. She had been there throughout those long drives to work in the winter without ever complaining. I knew that I loved her.

And then, as the wedding day drew near, I fell ill, came down with shingles. That morning, when I looked in the bathroom mirror, I saw small bumps on my face and neck, and inside my mouth. I felt so ill I thought I was going to die. I wasn't really going to die. Just acted as if I was. It is so true what they say about men and being ill—we turn into big babies. Well I'm the biggest baby of all when I'm sick and so of course I exaggerated my condition and symptoms to Emma. I had to take more than a week off work. During that time I was mostly alone in my room and away from other people. But, even though Emma knew the risk of being close to someone with shingles, she visited me daily and kept me company.

November 14, 2009: that's day we became husband and wife. Seeing her walking down that aisle sent chills down my spine. Some people said afterwards that I was crying like a baby. At first, I denied it. But who was I kidding? I was crying like a *big* baby. The feeling of being loved and belonging to someone was too over-whelming. All my life I had tried to prove myself to others. I had longed for some sort of validation from others and had looked for someone to just love me for me. I felt now that I would no longer have to have such feelings ever again.

Growing up, I wasn't really the type to pursue women and, quite frankly, I really didn't want to. I was always trying to keep my eyes on some sort of goal in my life and I felt that women were just a distraction. But the reality was that I had very low self-esteem. The stuttering that I struggled with as a young boy deflated most of my dreams and ambitions. The loneliness at home, the absence of my father and the missing family connection played a huge part in how I saw myself. But then there was this woman, walking down the aisle wearing all white and she couldn't care less about my weaknesses and flaws. She just loved me for me.

After the wedding and honeymoon, we purchased a house in Stouffville, north of Toronto. Living there added an extra 45 minutes to my work day but we thought at the time that purchasing property was the right move for us. We thought about raising a family in that home and, despite the extra travel time for myself and Emma, we made the decision to move. However, Emma and Iquickly realized that it wasn't the right move to make. We tried to arrange some sort of travelling system that best fit our work time needs. Since the majority of my work shift was long splits, we had worked out that I would take her to her mother's house in the morning and then head to work myself.

Sounds easy, right? Not really. I usually started work around 5:00 am and finished around 6:00 pm. So in order to get to work on time and drop Emma at her mother's house, I had to wake up around 3:00 am. Since we only had one car at the time and it wasn't feasible for us to purchase another, we had to leave our home around 4:00 am. Every morning when that alarm clock went off my heart broke because there was Emma fast asleep. I knew that

I would have to wake her up. But before doing that I would make sure that her clothes for work were in the car and that whatever she needed to get ready at her mom's was there for her. When it was the cold and the car was freezing, I would wake up extra early, go to the car and cover the passenger seat with a thick blanket. Despite the sacrifice that was made in this arrangement, she didn't complain once about the bad decision I had made to move.

I was physically and mentally exhausted with the early mornings and working long days because of the split shift. Months went by where I would miss family events, miss friends getting together and parties, and miss time with Emma. Over time the connection between Emma and I started to fade. I began to resent my job — not because of the job itself, but because the hours I was working were not compatible with Emma's. It is extremely difficult to continue a relationship with someone when all the communication is through the phone or via text. On my long breaks during the split shifts, instead of going into the car to sleep, I would go to a nearby park and cry.

Here I was with such a great job opportunity, a great salary, a great wife and family and I felt as if I was a nobody again. As if I was going nowhere in life. As if I had so much to carry on my shoulders without having the strength to do so. The constant fatigue because of the long days and the negative comments from passengers added to the lowering of my self-esteem. Without realizing it, I was sinking lower and lower into depression. I thought very seriously about quitting. Thoughts about my past starting to creep up. Thoughts about how well I had been treated when I was playing basketball. Thoughts about the passion I had for playing basketball. Thoughts about how I was now being treated. Did I really want to stay in a job that literally took up my whole life?

Was this job for me—the long hours, the varying off days, the pressures from the public and the losing of friends? Was this job really for me?

One night Emma and I watched a movie called *The Blindside*. It was basically a movie about a teen boy being given an opportunity to get a football scholarship with the help of a family. A dream come true.

At the end of the movie, an avalanche of emotions rose up in me and I had an emotional breakdown. Watching this movie took me right back to what I had actually lived through in my own life. But, instead of fulfilling my dreams, I was being yelled at by the public while driving a TTC bus. Emma knew something was wrong with me as I sat there in silence, tears flowing down my cheeks. I went upstairs to be alone. When I didn't return, Emma came searching for me and found me in the bedroom closet crying. I was at the lowest point of my life. I was unappreciated at work, unappreciated by the public and felt as if I was unappreciated at home. I had no social life, no goals to pursue and even being a husband started to seem impossible for me. That night I changed.

I was overwhelmed by the heavy feeling of failure. I felt as if I had failed as a husband with the many mornings waking up Emma in order to get to work on time. Yes, I had a little bit of seniority but the work that I was able to choose from wasn't the greatest. Despite the number of new operators that were being hired, it seemed like the shifts that available to me were getting worse. In order to have some time with Emma, I took the shifts that started early. But that early morning travelling really dampened my spirits. I felt as if I was failing her by creating unnecessary hardships within our marriage. That night, all of the suppressed, bottled-up feelings from negative experiences whether at home or work erupted. I was sinking below the raging waters with no life jacket and, though Emma tried her best to save me, it was to no avail. The smile that once stretched across my face was now a frown. The happiness and positive attitude had turned into sadness and emptiness.

I was 25 when this happened, but I had changed so much that my wife no longer recognized me. Slowly and surely the connection between us splintered and the intimacy started to slip away. The love that we once cherished—and others admired—was turning into that between two friends, not two lovers. It was during this time that more and more female passengers started to introduce themselves to me. This hadn't happened to me before. Or it had and I hadn't paid any attention. But during this low time of my life, hearing such smooth words from these female passengers started to affect me. My affection towards my wife was decreasing and my mind was drawn towards the words of these other women.

We moved house a few times in order to get closer to work, and we fought to salvage our marriage. However, the lure and temptation of these women was too much, and I began to think that the grass was greener on the other side. Emma knew that there was something changing and that my feelings were not connected with her as they used to be. I was an emotional wreck. The demons from the past hadn't gone away. They had simply been waiting for the opportune time to take a hold of me again. Separation was looming over us and, despite the fact that we moved closer to the city to get away from the hectic commuting, it didn't really smooth out the edges of the relationship.

At 27, I was officially divorced and living back at home with my mother. I was feeling distressed and broken and I coped with this the same way that I had done when my dad left home. I started to isolate myself from everyone: my family, my friends and my work colleagues. My work life suffered dramatically. It didn't really matter to me anymore what the public's opinion of me was and I didn't really pay any attention to the insignificant complaints that they had. I just wanted to be left alone. So I started to work the graveyard shift permanently.

WALKING IN THE SHOES OF A TRANSIT OPERATOR VI

Author: *How has being a transit operator affected your romantic life, your relationships?*

Operator 1:   *What people don't really understand is that shift work can be dramatically paralyzing for a relationship. Obviously it helps if the person is understanding and knows that the shifts that we get often times consume the majority of the day. I have seen plenty of operators date only people who work a shift pattern also because they understand the difficulties that shift works comes with. I have dated and many of the partners that I got couldn't handle the shifts that I was doing until I met a nurse. It is truly difficult to maintain a healthy relationship if the other person is not understanding.*

Operator 2:   *I have been married for 12 years now and the whole secret to staying married as an operator is to go straight home to your wife when your shift is done. I am not kidding. Yes, it is good to create friendships and bond with your buddies but time spent with your work buddies could be time spent with your wife. I am already away from her sometimes 12-13 hours per day. She knows that, when I can, I am coming home to her.*

Operator 3:   *I have been married for four years now and we have a beautiful daughter and yes shift work does suck but I take every opportunity I can to be with them. They come first, second and third. A lot of operators, especially men, when they see a lot of beautiful women taking the transit system, forget to realize what they have at home.*

Operator 4: Twenty-five years together with my wife but been married for 20 years and let me tell you it has its ups and downs but we are still strong. I know that this company has a very high divorce rate. It is really hard to maintain a relationship due to the shifts and schedules. But my wife and I knew when I first started as a TTC operator what we were getting ourselves into and we stuck it out. Now in our later life, our love for each other has never been sweeter and more beautiful than ever. We went through a lot at the beginning of my TTC career and there have been plenty of opportunities to cheat with the women who come on the bus but at the end of the day is it really worth it?

Operator 5: I am not going to pretend like I am some angel. I have been married a few times and all of my marriages ended in divorce. When I got this job being an operator it was like the women came out of the woodwork. At the end of shifts often times I would receive phone numbers written on transfers and given to me. What made it so tempting to engage and entertain are these long shifts being away from home. It was like my work became my life and my home was just a place to stay. Do I regret it? Of course I regret my actions cheating with these individuals but walk in my shoes and you will see how difficult it truly is.

Operator 6: For me personally the reason why I am single and don't really want to get married is because on this job it is so unfair for the other spouse. I am sure you have heard from operators the many stories of divorce and cheating. It is everywhere. When I was in a committed relationship, my dating partner really couldn't handle my having to on *weekends and holidays and missing events. The individual constantly complained about not being able to spend time with me but there was nothing that I could do. So I stay single and just enjoy life.*

Operator 7:   *I have been married for little over three years now and I have such an understanding wife who knows all about shift work and the constant exposure to women. There are female passengers who give their numbers to me all the time, but I pay no attention to them because it will only lead to the divorce court. However, the fact that I am married doesn't really prevent female passengers from offering their numbers to me. In fact, it draws them even more.*

Operator 8:   *As a female operator, I have been married for over 10 years and there have been plenty of opportunities to cheat on my husband. I would say it is a daily thing for a male passenger to offer to take me out or buy me a drink on my off day. It was flattering at first but over time it is really bothersome. My husband knows everything and it is amazing that he is so understanding.*

Operator 9:   *As a married man it is really difficult being exposed to such large numbers of women on a daily basis. I have never cheated, but there have been plenty of opportunities to do so. I don't know any male operators who haven't been through a divorce. I am sure there are some out there, but I haven't met one personally.*

Operator 10:   *There are operators who shoot themselves in the foot by sleeping around and cheating on their wives. When they get caught, the wives take them to the cleaners and take all that they own. But it is not just men who cheat on their spouses on this job. There are women who do it too. It is really bad.*

Operator 11: *I totally believe that there are women out there who target TTC guys. They try to lure them because of the benefits and other perks that we get through this job. I had a woman say to me straight in my face that she had three children by three different men and that the oldest child was coming off child support. So she was looking for a TTC operator to have a child with so that she could replenish the money that she would lose once the benefits ended for the eldest child.*

Operator 12: *It is pretty sad to see so many divorces within the TTC. The secret truly is to spend as much time with your family when you have free time. Don't let the shift hours or the put downs from the public consume your life. I am not married or in a relationship and really and truly I really don't want to be in one. I only have a few years on the job and I feel like my life is my job because I am at work more than home. Being at work 12 hours per day gives me little time to adequately develop a relationship.*

Operator 13: *I have been married for 15 years now. That's because, as soon as I am done, I go straight home to my family. There are so many temptations to stay and chat with the guys but I spend the majority of the day at work and little time at home. I can't let my time with my family slip away and miss the important stuff with my kids.*

Operator 14: *I have been married for 10 years and my husband knows exactly the type of work that I'm involved in. He knows that I get given phone numbers and that my schedule is not from 9 to 5. He's a very understanding and supportive man and we have a lovely relationship.*

Operator 15: *I cheated on my spouse many times. We are not together any more of course but while we were together the overwhelming emotional connection from many female passengers was extremely high. When I had an arguments at my home with my wife, I would come to work and all I saw was beautiful women coming on to me and saying sweet things to me I fell. This job is truly dangerous for married men because of the beautiful women that we see on a daily basis.*

Operator 16: *Yes, I get numbers from guys everyday but I really do love my husband and I wouldn't trade what I have for the world. At the beginning, after getting my job, my relationship with my husband was very different because we had to adjust our lives due to the shifts that I was getting. The times that we spent together before work decreased hugely because I was working midnights. But my husband was great and knew that I had to get my rest during the day. He made all the necessary arrangements for me to sleep during the day, as well as cooking all the meals for the family to eat. Working as an operator, you will lose time spent with your family and friends but that is the sacrifice that is made.*

Operator 17: *When people see the TTC uniform on a man or woman, the first thing that goes through their minds are dollar signs. So many men have fallen to the enticement of* *females on this job and are now paying for it. It is very difficult being a man on this job because you see beautiful women all day, every day. However, there are men on this job who stay faithful to their wives, and I salute them.*

Operator 18: *It is sometimes a very lonely job and so it always seems when you are at your lowest point in life that the temptation comes in a form of a woman saying sweet words. I cheated on my wife and till this day I regret it. No excuse, but the long hours away from home were definitely a factor for me doing what I did.*

Operator 19: *My wife didn't want to deal with the long shifts that I used to do and so I tried to work schedules that fit her schedule. We have been married for 12 years now and things are great. You just have to learn and communicate everything to her and through her because at the end of the day the working life affects the home life.*

Operator 20: *Yes, I did cheat on my husband. When I was getting numbers from men on a daily basis, it was easy to find comfort in them when things weren't going well at home. Being a public figure in a small way attracts attention whether unwanted or wanted. During a huge fight between my husband and me, I cheated. It isn't something I am happy about but often times because of our opposite shifts I wouldn't see my husband for a few days at a time. We are divorced now and I probably won't get married again.*

Author: *What about when you hear anger and frustration from the passengers? How has that affected you?*

Operator 21: *I have been an operator for five years and I am not going to lie. I have changed very much. I didn't mean to or want to change for the worse but sometimes being an operator feels like I am human punching bag. No matter how much the TTC caters to people, they are never satisfied. I know I am categorizing the small minority of passengers who cause the most trouble but it just seems like everyone is against us. We definitely have a bad name and reputation amongst the public, even though not all operators are bad. I am tired of hearing the complaints from the public.*

Operator 22: *As an operator you are stuck between a rock and a hard place. You cannot control and please everyone no matter how hard you try. There could be a blizzard outside and you could have easily called in sick but you decide to go to work. You push through the snow and get to work only to hear passengers complaining and mumbling because the bus you are driving is late by a few minutes.*

Operator 23: *In total I have nine years on the job. I have seen the good, the bad and the ugly from people and it has turned me off people, even when I am not working. I remember, in my fourth year on the job, a gentleman stood up and charged to the front of the streetcar as I passed a stop on Bathurst. He turned to me and said: "You know you are a fucking idiot. You passed my stop!" I explained to him that he didn't pull the cord or give me any indication that he wanted that stop. The passenger continued to use profanity and got so boisterous that he didn't really take in the fact that there were children on the streetcar going home from school. I reminded him that, for next time, he should* *give the operator some sort of notice that he wanted the next stop. He finally got off the streetcar but not without throwing the f-bomb my way a few more times. How do you think that would make anyone feel? And I was just doing my job.*

Operator 24: *I have over 20 years on the job and I remember when I first started working telling my wife to never ask me about work when I got home. At work sometimes I feel very degraded and low because for the most part we get the brunt of it from the public when something goes wrong with the transit system.*

Operator 25: *Many people think that being an operator is easy and that we are nothing but lazy individuals. I remember a passenger actually saying to my face how I wasn't worth the wage that I was receiving because all I did was sit and drive all day. The amount of things that we actually do is way more than just driving. But just hearing things like that really does make me feel so unappreciated and undeserving of what I have with this job.*

Operator 26: *It does affect you when you hear such vulgar language over and over again. I started to change who I was, and I developed a hard heart towards the public. Over time I turned into someone who I didn't even recognize. For years I lived with this mindset until I realized that having a hard hearted approach towards people was not doing anyone any good, particularly me. This job can change you if you let it, and I have seen plenty of operators who have fallen into such a trap.*

What lies behind you and what lies in front of you,
pales in comparison to what lies inside of you.
—Ralph Waldo Emerson

CHAPTER 6

===

RISE OF THE PHOENIX

During those times following my divorce, many thoughts, mostly negative, would creep in my mind. Isolation from family and friends made sense to me. Feelings of being just another divorce statistic and feeling as if I couldn't go on weighed heavily on me. The reputation that I had strived to build, that of a man of integrity, loyalty and devotion, was tumbling down around me. I thought about how being a divorced man would tarnish me for life. I felt as if I was standing on quicksand and slowly, day by day, sinking lower and lower emotionally.

Many people tried to reach out to me, to offer me counsel and wisdom. But it was as if I wasn't ready to move on from that emotional state. At work, I didn't socialize much with co-workers or staff and, because I was on the graveyard shift, there weren't many passengers on my bus at any one time. It was a very lonely period in my life. I had retreated into my "inner cave" just as I had done in the days after my dad left me.

But one night, in my room pondering on my life, I came across an old journal that I had written when I was 15 years old. In that journal the young boy that was someone full of goals and ambition, ready to take on the world. Throughout the pages were inspirational quotes and stories of individuals who conquer their fears and triumph over adversity. While reading, tears would flow down my cheeks as I pictured that little boy and the man that I had become. I missed the innocence of that boy. I missed the purity of life and passion of that boy. I wanted to get it back. A spark formed in my heart that night. A spark to get on a journey that would lead to growth and personal improvement as a man.

I started to read the books that I had on character and leadership and started to believe once more in the idea of bettering myself. I filled my mind with books on people who, in the face of failure, had triumphed and had an amazing story to share with others. This inspired me and I finally saw a ray of hope. I came across one book in particular that changed the way I thought about myself and the situation I was in: *Think and Grow Rich* by Napoleon Hill. I began to realize that, despite being in such a slump, mainly because of my actions, I could change my situation by changing the way I thought about things.

Here I was focusing on how bad my job was because I felt it was the cause of my failed marriage. I was focusing on how bad my life was because I wasn't really close to my family or friends. I was focusing on the belief that I had wasted the majority of my life. Reading such books, I started to see and understand how the way I was thinking about myself wasn't producing anything good in me. Dwelling on negative situations wasn't cultivating a winner's attitude towards my personal and work life.

Instead, I forced myself to focus on my interior and who I was as a person. I changed how I viewed myself and, as a result, my views of other people changed as well. While driving the bus, I started to work every shift as if the CEO was standing right beside me. I would speak to myself and encourage myself to be the best I could be—first as a man and then as an operator. Despite the fact that I had nothing to show materially for the years I had worked, I had something higher in value than what money could buy. I had the knowledge that I was in control of what happens to the inside of me, the real me, not my circumstances, environment or the people around me. Instead of seeing a frown on passengers when they got on my bus, it was a smile that greeted them. Despite the fact that nothing changed on the outside—I was still divorced, still not close with my family and friends, there was a change on the inside.

I started seeing myself and life in a whole different light. I started to see my work in a different way as well, not just a source of income but also an opportunity to have an impact on everyone with whom I came in contact. I saw the importance of being a bus driver. I was driving people home to their families, driving students to their schools, driving workers to work. I started to see the importance of what I did even if these people themselves didn't see it. I began to love my job, began to love interacting with the customers. I loved the fact that, as a bus driver, I could be a counsellor, a guide, a teacher, and have the ability to create a lasting impression upon everyone that I met.

My eyes were opening up to the fact that passengers are people and not just numbers to transport. I started to notice many things that I didn't even see before as I was too focused on myself and my own problems. One night I was working the graveyard shift. It was around 1:00 am when a young lady boarded the bus. She paid and quietly sat down in the seat that was closest to the front door. Her eyes were puffy, her shirt was soaked and her eyes was red. It was apparent that she had been crying before she got on the bus and she had wiped her tears on her shirt. My heart broke when I heard her weeping again as she sat there alone. She was the only passenger on the vehicle and so her weeping sounded like she was shouting. It almost echoed around the big empty bus.

I asked her what was wrong and told her that I was all ears if she wanted to talk. Sometimes all someone needs is a listening ear. I had a long way to go to get to the end of the route, which was where she was going as well. Slowly she began to share her story. She was a recovering drug addict who had been addicted to cocaine for several years but she had been clean for a long time. But then she said that she had slipped into the addiction again. She told me that she had no family in Toronto. All she had was her boyfriend who wasn't really happy when she was clean. It was apparent that he was using her for her body and someone with whom to get high. She wept as she told her story.

I could tell that she desperately wanted to escape the stranglehold of the drugs but she felt like she had no one to turn to because her family lived outside of Canada. I just listened as she released the burden of her story. Then we finally reached the end of the route to the subway station. For the entire time that she had been on the bus, she had done the majority of the talking. But I had seen her countenance change after sharing everything that was going on in her life with someone. I told her to look into getting professional help and I wished her well.

The job of a TTC operator is not only to operate a transport vehicle on a designated route. There are many times when the operators step up and take on other forms of "duties" in order to assist the passengers. I remember working an evening shift one time when a lady and her child, coming from the local zoo, got on the bus. It was a busy route and, after a few stops, the bus was beginning to get crowded. I noticed an older man who sat right beside the child. I felt very uneasy about the way he was positioning himself against her and talking to her. I also noticed the mother looking very uncomfortable but I could tell that she was a little timid and that she didn't want to say anything to the man. He was a big guy and looked like a football player.

There was no way that I could just ignore the situation and drive the bus. I called the man up to the front and tried to engage him in a friendly conversation. We talked about the weather, about his life and soon he was so into our conversation that, by the time we finished talking, the bus had arrived at Kennedy station, the end of the route. The man got off and, as the rest of the bus was emptying, the child's mother came up to me. The bus was completely empty now and it was just the three of us and I could see that the woman was a little teary eyed. She thanked me for removing the man away from her daughter. She said that she had wanted to say something to him but was afraid because he looked emotionally unstable. Hearing the thanks from the lady gave me such a positive energy and that feeling kept me going for the remainder of my shift.

By no means am I sharing these stories to say that I am special, or deserving of an award. But what the public doesn't see or hear about are exactly these stories. Stories about operators who go above and beyond their job requirements every single day. Operators who are constantly aware of the dangers, either to them or to the public, and have acted swiftly to avert tragic consequences, simply by spotting the potential impact of situations they see developing.

I just have a couple of questions for anyone who is a regular user of the transit system: When was the last time that you thanked your TTC operator for getting you to your destination in a safe manner? When was the last time that you just said a simple "Thank You"? The next time you get on a TTC vehicle, try acknowledging the person who is driving and show your appreciation to them. There are so many things that can go wrong in such a short time while operating a large vehicle, but they don't happen because of the keen eye and quick response of the operator. So even if the TTC vehicle is late picking you up, whether due to traffic, due to volume of passengers, or an accident, saying "thank you" to the operator can go a long way, perhaps a lot further than you realize.

> *God gave you a gift of 86,400 seconds today.*
> *Have you used one to say: Thank you?*
> —William A. Ward

Any hardworking spouse can relate to this. You come home from a hard day at work, having spent all of your energy and efforts trying to make that sale, and your partner whispers that he or she is thankful for all that you do for the family. How wonderful that makes you feel, how those simple two words can give you such an energy boost. You feel loved and appreciated and you know that your efforts are not going unnoticed. What am I trying to say by using these examples? That words have power. That what we say can have a dramatic influence on the person on the receiving end.

As an operator myself for six years, my heart was always made light when I would go out of my way to provide the best customer service possible and then receive a thank you. But the opposite is very true as well. My heart would be crushed little by little when I would go out of my way and, instead of getting a thank you, I would get silence or disrespect. Not that I was doing things in order to get praise, but I felt the difference between when I was being treated nicely by the public and when I was being treated as if I didn't exist. The TTC has many caring operators who deserve the highest praise for going above and beyond the line of duty. This needs to be acknowledged by the public. An acknowledgement that the operator is a fellow a human being is definitely a good start.

Being a TTC bus driver is just the visible surface of who I am as an individual. When I realized I was a human being and began to understand my own value and self-worth, I also started to take my job very seriously and learned to love everything about it. The more I took my eyes off of myself, the more I saw the concerns in others, the pain in others, and saw that passengers are humans too. The more I reached out and looked to others and found ways to bring a smile to their faces, the more my own smile became larger and larger. The problems that I thought were overwhelming started to become less and less significant as I saw others with greater problems. I also saw that I had the opportunity to bring relief simply through my presence as a bus operator.

As I started to get to know more of the regular passengers, many would open up to me and share their lives. I loved to listen but it also saddened me at times to hear the stories. Many had to work two to three jobs just to make ends meet. I saw construction workers sleeping on the bus because of the early morning work shifts that they had to endure. During the winter on my overnight shifts, I would get those who would ask me if they could take shelter on the bus even if just for a few hours because they couldn't afford anything else.

On my graveyard shifts, I met an older lady who boarded the bus every night after her shift at Tim Hortons. I would purposely wait for her at the nearby stop because I knew that, if she didn't catch my bus, she would have to wait nearly half an hour for the next one. Every time she got on, she would softly say "thank you" and would sit down in utter exhaustion. After talking to her many nights in a row for weeks on end, she had opened up to me. I learned she had no family and was all by herself. We became good friends. She would always bring me candies and she is someone that I still think about to this day.

Fellow TTC operators and transit operators all over the world, we have the power to touch so many lives. We can be a source of encouragement and happiness to everyone with whom we come into contact. We are a very fortunate group of individuals and should always remember that we are in control of who we are. Why not be an agent of gratitude towards others? Why not be an agent of kindness towards others?

At 28 years old, I had completed nearly seven years on the job and was really enjoying it again. I was still working overnights but not because I wanted to get away from people, but because I got accustomed to it. One day, as I was walking to the division at the end of my shift, I saw a job opening for "supervisor" on the notice board. I had never given much thought to becoming a supervisor. I loved being a TTC operator but there was an itch in me to try and grow within the company. Amongst the drivers inside the division, there was much chatter about this job opening.

While driving during the night, the thought of being a supervisor would pop up in my mind periodically but I would brush it off. Night by night that thought would re-enter until I began to dwell on it and day dream about it. The possibility of building a greater scope of character within me, the possibility of having a greater range of influence amongst others and to be able to touch lives in a greater measure intrigued me. I wanted to take on the challenge. I wanted something to strive for and this job opening came at the right time. The thought of becoming a supervisor literally consumed my mind and I set my heart to accomplish this goal.

I updated my resume and applied for the position before the deadline expired, thinking that I had nothing to lose and much to gain. Time passed with no word from the human resources department or my manager about the job. But I still had faith that I would get it. I was at the gym a few days later when my phone rang. It was a TTC manager stating that I had an interview for the supervisor position. What a joyous moment! I felt as though I could lift the heaviest weight without any trouble. I was on top of the world and I quickly called my mom to tell her the great news.

The night before the interview, I was working an overnight shift. I suddenly realized that the TTC manager had not specified if the interview was in the morning or evening. I assumed that it would be 6:00 pm since my shift ended around 5:30 am and a 6:00 am interview wouldn't give me enough time to prepare myself. Nevertheless, the whole night as I was driving, I was troubled about the time of the interview. It would have been a tragedy if I missed the interview because it actually was in the morning. It was around 5:15 am when I got back to my home division. I called the location that the interview was being held. To my amazement, it was set for 6:00 am! From my division to my house was normally a 25-minute drive and from my house to the interview location was 15-minute drive. By the time I got to my car it was 5:30, leaving me little time to prepare for the interview. But I wanted this job more than anything. I couldn't let anything get in my way.

I cut the time from work to home in half, and got there in less than 15 minutes. My mom and I lived on the 11th floor of the apartment building and, when I got to the lobby, none of the elevators were working! But not even the disabled elevators would stop me from getting to this interview on time. I took to the stairs. Running up 11 flights of stairs early in the morning was no easy task but it did shake off the tired feeling that I had at the end of a long shift. I had no time to properly shave, no time to take a shower or to attempt to improve my appearance. The only thing I had time to do was to put on my suit, this time a new suit. Down I went on the stairs and running to my car. I only had 10 minutes to get to the interview and I knew that the TTC is very strict on time and time management.

Brushing my teeth and tying my shoes while driving a manual car wasn't easy. But I was so close and I didn't want to be late. I made it to the interview location in five minutes, leaving me with five minutes left. I ran towards the entrance while trying to feed my belt through my pants and fasten it. I made it. I took a deep breath. I made it.

When the interview was over, I knew I had tried my best and had no regrets in applying. I was thankful for the opportunity even just to get an interview for the supervisory position. The thing about working for TTC that I loved the most was the potential for growth and the opportunity to do so and I will forever be in debt towards this company for what it has given me.

A few weeks went by before I got the phone call stating that I had the job. No words can express how grateful I was that the TTC was taking this chance on me. I vowed to be the best supervisor I could be and to learn as much as I could. Throughout my life I've gone through trials and tribulations but it was those experiences that allowed me to mature emotionally and intellectually. Here I am now, a 29-year-old supervisor at the time of writing this book. I love every inch of my job and the opportunity to have a positive influence on my colleagues and every TTC operator with whom I come in contact. I have nothing but admiration towards the frontline workers because I was once in the same trenches and, in a sense, still am.

WALKING IN THE SHOES OF A TRANSIT OPERATOR VII

Author: *What other duties have you performed at work in order to assist passengers?*

Operator 1: *I remember getting to a certain station and seeing an elderly man really having a hard time making his way around. One by one people would bypass him. It was the morning rush hour and there was the usual mad surge of people trying to get to work on time. I couldn't just watch and do nothing, so I took the man all the way down to where the subway platform was and made sure he was heading in the right direction.*

Operator 2: *I take pride and joy in being a kind operator. I make it my mission to try to put a smile on every face that boards the vehicle that I am driving. I say hi and smile at every single person. I've noticed that a simple smile can make someone's day.*

Operator 3: *There are many times people would accidentally leave personal belongings on the TTC vehicle. I remember when I got to the end of the route one time, I noticed a wallet that had been left. I could only imagine what the person who left it on the vehicle must have been thinking. A text from the supervisor went out to all the TTC vehicles on that particular route asking if someone found a wallet. Needless to say, with the help of the supervisor, we got the wallet back to the owner and just seeing the thankfulness on that person's face made my day.*

Operator 4: *There was an elderly lady who came onto the vehicle with a lot of groceries. Unfortunately one of her bags broke and several things fell to the floor. There were not many people onboard, but no one seemed to be inclined to help. I just got out of my seat and helped the lady. Even just offering a helping hand like this goes a long way but will never get recognized nor do I want to be recognized for this. However, I was a little upset to see not one person on the TTC vehicle willing to assist me.*

Operator 5: *It was raining, the type of rain that is so heavy you really cannot see in front of you. While driving the bus I noticed a lady with her stroller trying to get out of the rain but there wasn't any shelter for another few blocks. So I pulled over because I felt really bad that she and the stroller were getting soaked. I asked if she wanted a ride to wherever she was going and she was so grateful.*

Operator 6: *When I was finishing my shift, I got off the bus to head home only to see a blind person exiting the bus with me. He was asking people for directions but no one was assisting him so he stopped just a few yards in front of me. I went up to him and asked him if he needed help. He wanted to go to Wal-Mart but he was new to the area. He just needed to get there and then he said he would be fine. So I told him that I would help him if he would just put his hands around my arm. We talked on the way to Wal-Mart, but because I walked him to where he wanted to go, I missed my bus to go home. I didn't mind at all because I was very happy to help.*

Operator 7:   *There are simple things that many operators do that the public take for granted. All the times operators wait for the runners when they really don't have to. What about the times when operators make sure that the safety of all passengers is top priority when there is an unruly or drunken passenger? So many small gestures that will never make the news, but operators do them on a daily basis.*

Operator 8:   *I remember when I was at work and a pregnant lady got on and, for some reason, no one wanted to offer her a seat. It was in the morning rush hour and the TTC vehicle was packed but there are common courtesies that can't be overlooked. So I stopped the vehicle and announced if someone would be willing to offer up his or her seat for this pregnant woman. Finally after a few moments someone did. Courtesy is always a big part of our job even if it means having to go the extra mile.*

*I'm not concerned with your liking
or disliking me ... all I ask is that
you respect me as a human being.*
—Jackie Robinson

CHAPTER 7

———

SHOUT TO
THE MOUNTAIN TOPS!

*Think twice before you speak, because your words
and influence will plant the seed of either success
or failure in the mind of another.*

—Napoleon Hill

With the number of people that TTC frontline workers are exposed to, you can imagine the positive and negative feedback the operators receive. A friend of mine, also a new supervisor, and I were walking down Bathurst street, talking and discussing our future, dreams and goals. We were just enjoying the moment and saying how grateful we were to have been given this opportunity by the TTC. A man was walking in the opposite direction towards us. We didn't really pay any attention to the him, until we noticed that he was staring right at us. The man started to pull a face as if he wasn't happy about something, and he walked directly into our path causing us to stop right in front of him. He looked at of us, noticed the supervisory hats on our heads, the suits that we were wearing with the supervisor tag on and our black shining shoes. Then he yelled: "You guys don't deserve that job. You guys get paid way too much."

After yelling at us, he just continued on his journey, occasionally looking back over his shoulder. Here was a man who didn't know us. Did he just assume that this job had been handed to us on plate and that we hadn't had to work hard for it? Perhaps he thought that, because of our skin colour, we weren't deserving of such positions. Who knows? Whatever the reason for his random outburst, it was apparent that he was a very ignorant person. He didn't see the hardships I'd gone through and the tough lessons that I learned. He didn't see the valleys in my life, only my present mountain top situation. Too many people just see the climax of the operator's story. Yes, TTC operators get paid well, and that the benefits and pension are top notch. But, you never know what someone has gone through to get to where they are.

Throughout my driving career with the TTC, I have gone through many different experiences and I have many stories about dealing with the public. Dealing with the public is no easy task and as one operator said: "How uncommon common sense really is!" We live in a day and age where awareness of workplace harassment, bullying, and the mistreatment of others have changed the way companies deal with these issues. The TTC does an excellent job promoting and offering courses that the frontline workers have to take in order to deal with such mistreatment amongst co-workers. Courses that educate employees to be aware of the bullying and harassment at its beginning stages so the proper authorities can be called to stunt such behaviour.

As a supervisor, many operators have told me that the negative experiences I went through were also experienced by them, especially the abuse that occurs in their daily working lives. This chapter is dedicated to letting the public read for themselves detailed accounts of the abuse and assaults that TTC operators and supervisors undergo at the hands of unruly, drunken and often dangerous passengers. The first part of the chapter relates stories directly from the TTC website. In the second part, operators themselves tell their stories regarding situations that they have actually faced on the job.

Think about the bank teller who gets an earful because the bank can't cash the cheque that the customer wants until a certain day. Think about the verbal abuse police officers receive when a speeding ticket is issued to a motorist who is actually speeding. Think about any job that deals with the public and how one negative customer can literally ruin the day of the employee. The man who swore at me that night at the bus ruined my night and, if it wasn't for that sweet lady supervisor, I would have definitely resigned there and then. To the readers: I hope that, as you read these stories, you will begin to walk in the shoes of an operator for just a short time, and appreciate what really goes on behind the scenes every day.

TTC Website:
Jail Sentences Handed Down
for Assaults on TTC Employees

On January 11, a male was involved in a verbal dispute with other passengers on a King streetcar. The streetcar operator intervened and was assaulted by the male and threatened with death. The suspect fled, and was later arrested by members of Toronto Police Services. On january 16, Ryan Sheppard, 28, pleaded guilty to assault and was sentenced to 30 days in jail.

On January 14, a woman boarded a King streetcar without paying a fare. When the operator requested a fare, she spat in his face, and slapped him. Toronto police arrested the woman a short time later. Asmait Gebre-Yohannes, 35, pleaded guilty to assault, and was sentenced to 44 days in jail and one year's probation.

On January 8, two transit enforcement officers were performing proof of payment duties on the Wueen streetcar. A male boarded via the rear doors. The officers asked for proof of payment. The male became uncooperative, then spat in both officer's faces. On

January 15, Allan Dorinie, 49, pleaded guilty to assault, and was sentenced to 68 days in jail and 18 months probation. His probation order prohibits him from all TTC vehicles and property for the first six months of his probation.

On January 28, a male boarded a TTC streetcar on Queen street and demanded a free ride. The streetcar operator refused to allow the free ride, at which time the male spat on the operator, verbally abused him and fled the scene. He was arrested by Toronto police a short distance away. On March 14, Sala Hussein, 56, pleaded guilty to a charge of assault, and was sentenced to 45 days in jail, and 18 months' probation.

On December 21, 2013, a man boarded a bus without paying fare near Lawrence Ave. E. and Kingston Rd. When the operator requested a fare, the suspect spat in his face and attempted to strike him with an umbrella. The operator was transported to hospital with mirror injuries. On January 16, Christopher Otoo, 21, pleaded guilty to a charge of assault and was sentenced to 60 days in jail and two years probation. As part of his probation order, Otoo is not allowed on TTC vehicles and property between 10 pm and 6 am, or with alcohol or non-prescription drugs in his system.

On Sept. 17, 2010, a man boarded a bus with an invalid transfer near Brimley Rd. and Steeles Ave. E. When the operator refused to accept the transfer, the man became enraged and removed a knife from his backpack, stabbing the operator three times in his leg and hand. The suspect fled the scene, but was arrested by Toronto police the next day and charged with attempted murder, aggravated assault with a weapon, possession of a weapon and carrying a concealed weapon. The assault was captured by CCTV on board the bus and was presented as evidence in court. The male was convicted of aggravated assault in March 2012. On Feb. 21, 2014, Wel Yang, 43, was sentenced to nine years in prison and an additional 10-year long-term supervision order after his prison sentence is served.

A 44-year-old man was sentenced to 45 days in jail and an 18-month ban from riding the subway for sexually assaulting a TTC transit ambassador. On August 4, (2014) at 3:25 pm, the accused approached the employee and asked for help. He then slid his hand in the victim's right pocket and groped her buttocks. The ambassador reported the incident and the male fled. Transit enforcement officers were dispatched to the scene and located the man at Dundas station. Following an investigation, he was arrested by Toronto police and charged with sexual assault. On August 20, Arshad Sajid entered a guilty plea to sexual assault. He was also fined $200, and has been ordered to pay $250 restitution to the victim.

September 19, 2014, a 21-year-old man was sentenced to 90 days in jail for assaulting a TTC bus operator. The man also received an additional 90 days for failing to comply with conditions of a recognizance order. On March 23, a male boarded a bus at Kingston rd. And Lawrence Ave. E. He was requested by the operator to lower the volume of music coming from his phone. The man complied. While arriving at his stop, the man approached the operator and commented about not knowing who the operator was dealing with. He then punched the operator several times in the head and face. With the aid of CCTV images from the bus, Toronto police arrested the suspect a short time later. Tyler brown, age 21, who was in custody serving time unrelated to this incident, pleaded guilty to assault and failure to comply with recognizance. He was sentenced to 90 days for each offence (180 total) to be served concurrently and following his current sentence. Brown was also placed on probation following his incarceration and ordered to stay away from the TTC operator. The employee received lacerations and contusions on his face and head.

On January 5, 2012, a 19-year-old man was sentenced to 21 days in jail, and banned from the TTC between 11 pm and 6 am for assaulting a TTC uniformed supervisor. On Dec. 29, just after midnight, a TTC supervisor was called to the Long Branch loop to check on the well-being of a man who had passed out on a streetcar. When the male was woken up he was found to be in possession of a half bottle of liquor. He was asked to leave the vehicle. Once off the streetcar, the man attempted to re-enter, spitting in the face of the supervisor. He continued to spit at the supervisor from the sidewalk. The man was arrested by Toronto police on the scene and charged with assault. On the morning of Dec. 29, at his bail hearing, 19-year-old Emmanuel Yihun entered a guilty plea to the assault charge. He also received 10 months' probation, and a ban from being on the TTC with any alcohol or illegal drugs in his system.

February 24, 2012, a 38-year-old man was sentenced to 20 days in jail for threatening death and possession of marijuana. On February 5, a male was in the TTC's Humber loop, demanding free rides from TTC operators, threatening to kill them if they did not comply. The suspect was arrested by officers from Toronto Police Service 22 division and held for a bail hearing. Vangeli Keskinov pleaded guilty to the charges. As well as the 20-day jail sentence, Keskinov was placed on probation for one year with a condition that he not be under the influence of alcohol or illegal drugs while on TTC vehicles or property.

March 13, 2012, a man gets 50 days in jail for assaulting a uniformed TTC supervisor. A 49-year-old man was sentenced to 50 days in jail for assaulting a TTC supervisor at Dundas Station on Jan. 18. The accused was attempting to gain entry into Dundas Station without paying a proper fare. A dispute ensued with the collector on duty. When a female supervisor attempted to intervene in the fare dispute, the suspect spat on her and threatened to fight the TTC employee. Toronto police from 52 division were called to the scene and arrested the suspect. On march 8, at College Park Courts, Emile Deguire, 49, pleaded guilty to assault. He was sentenced to 50 days in jail, time served.

April 26, 2012, two men sent to jail for assaulting TTC employees. The two men received jail sentences in connection with two separate assaults.

On April 17, a TTC route supervisor was performing her duties at Bathurst and Lakeshore, when a male approached her and spat in her face and mouth for an unknown reason. Toronto police were called at the scene, and the suspect was arrested. Ian Merkley, 59, had been charged 18 times previously for violating TTC by-law no. 1. On April 25, Merkley was sentenced to six days in jail on top of nine days already served, for a total of 15 days. He also received 18 months probation that includes a total ban from all TTC vehicles and premises.

WALKING IN THE SHOES OF A TRANSIT OPERATOR VIII

Author: *TTC operators experience a lot of interaction with the public. Share one of your stories.*

Operator 1:   *So I was doing this particular bus route and a little boy and his mother got on the bus. It was obvious that the little boy has a physical disability and so I took my time and lowered the bus. The little boy didn't have crutches. Judging from outward appearances, the mother didn't look well off financially but you could tell the love and care that she had for her son was worth more than anything in the world. So when they were getting off at the front of the bus, I again lowered the bus and told them to take their time. A man also wanted to get off and he saw his bus going in the direction he wanted. He pushed his way past the boy almost knocking him down to the floor on his way. The mother was furious and was about to open her mouth when the man turned around and said: "The boy should have exited at the back of the bus!" I was so vexed that I was close to tears.*

Operator 2:   *It was a very dark night and sometimes people don't realize how quiet these TTC vehicles can get and that you cannot stop one on a dime. I was operating along a route where a lot of people don't use the lights to cross the road but they use the right of way (where only TTC vehicles and no other vehicles travel) to get to the other side of the street. An old man stepped right out from nowhere in front of the vehicle and got hit. It was such a numbing feeling that came over me, a feeling that I can't describe but will* *never forget. Later I realized that he died at the point of impact.*

Operator 3: *I hit a guy when I was driving a couple of years ago. I was going westbound and another TTC vehicle was coming eastbound. So visualize that scenario. I was pulling up to the stop and the guy was looking the other way trying to catch the eastbound vehicle. He started to run across the road but before I could react my vehicle and the man collided. He spun around and I could see his eyes as he spun. I couldn't sleep for days after that, but thankfully he was alright.*

Operator 4: *When I see passengers running for the buses or streetcars, I get really bothered by it because many don't understand that these vehicles can't just stop in a second. They are huge vehicles to manoeuvre. There was an instance where I was coming to a crosswalk and no one was there waiting to walk. I am very cautious with crosswalks and lights because you just never know. As I was approaching the crosswalk and about to pass it, a man ran across the street just to cross over to the other side. Immediately my heart jumped and flashes of hitting him and potentially killing him flooded my mind. I was so angry at him and his foolish decision to just run across the street without pressing the button or giving any indication that he was going to cross.*

Operator 5: *I feel like that every day when people running down the streetcar tracks head first jumping on the platform to catch the streetcar that they want to catch. I am not going to reward that kind of behaviour. I am sorry. I leave them* *at the platform and hope they learn and understand what a dumb thing they did. But when I have to stop because there are other law abiding passengers who are waiting patiently for the streetcar and here comes the individual who is running down the streetcar tracks, I tell that individual what a bonehead move that was in risking his life just to catch a TTC vehicle. I give him a little talking to and hope he gets it through my little chastening.*

Operator 6:   *TTC operators face so much more stuff on the road than the average driver ever faces. Cyclists who don't obey the rules of the road, pedestrians who cross the street illegally and motorists who drive aggressively and try to overtake buses, streetcars and other cars. It can be such a stressful work day when these things happen all shift long. Once, when I was operating the TTC vehicle, I saw in the mirror a cyclist holding onto the vehicle with one hand. My heart raced because what if he fell off of his bike and got mowed over by the vehicle. I stopped the vehicle and he rode his bike ahead of me. I was so upset on what he did because he put his own life in danger and it would have been my fault at the end of it.*

Operator 7:   *I remember I had this one guy get on the vehicle I was driving and normally I don't enforce the fares but I educate, giving the people the benefit of the doubt. I would pick up the same guy day after the day, and he would give me the same excuse about not having the right fare or any fare at that matter. A few days went by until I challenged him and told him how graceful I have been for a few days and how unfair it is for the regular paying* customers. He started to curse and use profanity at me all because I wanted him to pay the $3 fare.

Operator 8: *Time flies! I have 18 years on the job and counting. I have a story for you. I was driving the vehicle and a passenger came rushing up to me from the back and tapped me on the shoulder. He indicated that someone at the back had opened the emergency window and was urinating out of the window. It is a little bit funny now saying this afterwards, but if the public only knew how much stuff like this actually goes on, they would be shocked.*

Operator 9: *Remember the times when the fares have increased? Who do you think the public turned on and complained to? The frontline workers are the first point of contact for the customers and the complaints and ridicule come in like a flood. I have had passengers speak to me in such a rude way because the vehicle was late and they have asked me; "Why are you late, don't you know I pay your salary?" I have had people say how we (operators) don't do anything but sit all day long. How would anyone react if they had to go through this verbal abuse? I am not saying that it happens on a daily basis, but it does happen often. I am literally at the mercy of the public.*

Operator 10: *I don't mind helping people out when they don't have the full fares but I always educate them about the fares and the cost of transit. Sometimes people just forget or misplace it but what I see more and more now is the fact that people expect free rides and will actually argue if the free ride is not granted. I remember when I was doing a* *streetcar route and I saw two guys getting on the back of the streetcar and one guy at the front. The man that got on at the front paid and asked for a transfer and so I gave it. I was coming to the end of the route and I saw the three of them talking to each other, devising a plan to get me to give them two free transfers even though they didn't pay. Both of them came up to the front and gave me the excuse that I forgot to give them a transfer. But I knew that these were the two men who didn't even pay but entered the streetcar from the back doors. I challenged them and explained to them how they didn't pay and that transfers are not issued out without the proper fare being placed in the fare box. One of the two walked away but the other one became so enraged that he grabbed the full booklet of transfers that I placed at the front of my control panel of the streetcar. Sometimes it is very difficult to properly do my job because it seems like the customer thinks that whatever he/she does is OK and that there are no repercussions.*

Operator 11: *I have 29 years on this job and I can honestly say that things have changed, the way people treat each other. It is sad because I love people and I try to treat everyone with respect but over the years unfortunately people have become very selfish and self-centered. I remember back in the day when giving up a seat to an elderly person wasn't even an issue, now it is rare that people do this. I hope I am not being too negative but even the way people treat operators has at times made me feel demoralized. Sometimes I feel sad inside because when things go wrong and it's out of my control the public wants someone to blame and guess who they blame? The TTC vehicle that shows*

up to assist in the crisis. I wish things could go back to
how they were before but this won't happen until the operators treat the public as people, and the public treat the
operators as people.

Operator 12: I have had a coffee thrown at me, a punch thrown at me,
and someone tried to spit at me but it hit the window.
That's the worst thing a person can do to another human
being, spit in his or her direction.

Operator 13: It is an epidemic. There are so many people who don't
pay the correct fares and it is the same people who get
mad that the fares increase. All you have to do is to stand
outside a subway station and you will see people walking
into the subway without paying. Even though there are
signs that state that there is a fine, it is usually ignored
and disregarded. I want to educate those who seem to not
pay but many times I feel intimated because I am a female
operator and I don't want to get assaulted.

Operator 14: I hate the fact that those who steal from the company by
purposely not paying the right fare really believe that they
pulled a fast one on me. I know I shouldn't take collecting
fares too serious because you never know what people
have on them these days. But at the same time I take pride
in my work and who I am as a driver. Seeing the mistreatment of the system does upset me.

Operator 15: I have had someone come on the vehicle that I was driving
and actually fight with me because I wouldn't accept the
transfer in his hand. The transfer was 4 days old.

Operator 16: *I don't normally overly concern myself with the fare box for I tend to give the benefit of the doubt to the passenger. But when someone puts a penny in and then expects to ride the route, it is like slapping my face and insulting my intelligence.*

Operator 17: *It is very hard to not take it personally when someone tries to pull a fast one when I am driving the TTC vehicle. Picture the same individuals trying to pull such things with other establishments and I guarantee you it wouldn't go right with them. It is theft, bottom line.*

Operator 18: *You know the worst thing another human being can do is to spit at another human being. There is no reason at all to stoop that low in expressing your disagreements with another by spitting at them. I had that happen to me twice on the job and I never knew just how angry I could get until that happened to me.*

Operator 19: *Well, it was one of those days when everything that could go wrong for me went wrong. The bus in front of me was out of service and it wasn't the best of weather on that particular day. So I was carrying extra passenger loads in the middle of rush hour. I came to a stop where a man entered the bus fuming because he had to wait a little longer than usual for the bus. I was trying my best to accommodate the passengers but there was only so much I could do. Anyway, the man started to curse at me and without any warning, threw his coffee at me. What went through my mind was the fact that I questioned if this job was worth being treated like this.*

Operator 20: *I have five years on the job now and Ii have seen so many passengers trying to scam by putting in fake tokens, fake metro passes and using transfers that are more than a few days old.*

Operator 21: *I love the TTC. The company as a whole is an amazing company to work for and with. But being a female and of a certain colour skin can be hard when you're dealing with certain people. I remember picking up a drunk guy, and I don't mind at all as long as they don't cause trouble. I had only one year on the job so I was stuck doing overnights and it was a very cold day so I wasn't going to leave people behind. This man came on the vehicle and sat down peacefully but was very drunk, you can just tell. During my shift, all I heard from his mouth were racist comments my skin colour but I didn't really pay any attention. It was his stop and as he was getting off, he turns to me and says: "How did a person like you, with your skin colour, get such a great job?"*

Operator 22: *You know the monthly passes that the TTC gives out? They are usually available a week or so before the beginning of the new month so people can have it ready to use when that month starts. Well I recall calling back a customer and asking him to show me the pass that he had quickly flashed at me. I know it wasn't even the same month but the next month pass and it wasn't even a day or two until the next month. So I educated him saying that he can't use that pass because it is not even the same month. He was so adamant about how wrong I was and that it was TTC's fault for giving out the pass so early.*

He became so angry for something that is so simple as using the right pass for the right month, or just pay the fare. It is really that simple.

Operator 23: *I remember on my third day at work driving an overnight route. I wasn't too nervous or anything so that wasn't an issue. But I remember while I was driving the Bloor night bus a huge commotion happening on the back of the bus. A passenger rushed to the front and said that a person was threatening someone else with a saw! On my third day this happened and I was a little nervous but dealt with the situation with boldness. I made the announcement on the PA system and said: "The police are coming please leave the vehicle!" The two guys quietly got off the vehicle and I went on with my shift. If the public only knew what operators actually go through they would be shocked.*

Operator 24: *Driving the subway is a little different than the surface vehicles because I don't have to deal with the public face to face. But sometimes being the guard of the train (the person that deals with the opening and closing of the train doors), there were times when people would try to slap my face or spit at me just because I had to close the door to allow the train to depart.*

Operator 25: *I remember instructing a man that he had to pay or else he would have to leave the vehicle. I had seen him on my bus many times and I had given him free rides before but this time I had to put my foot down. He got so upset that I didn't let him on for free, that he took all the transfers from the transfer holder and ran out. He stole all the* *transfers I had, just because he didn't want to pay for his ride.*

Operator 26: *It is very difficult taking pride in what you do when everyday someone is trying to defraud the system and trying to pull a fast one on you. It is like the same people that try and play the system countless times not knowing that the lost revenue needs to come from somewhere. You wonder why the fares keep on increasing.*

Operator 27: *People have changed tremendously. Today's world is a very self-centered one. In 22 years on this job, I have gone through two decades observing and talking to millions of people. I remember long ago that I was able to settle down unruly passengers, calm down escalating situations on my own. But nowadays you have to be so careful because you just don't know what someone has on them these days or what they might do.*

Operator 28: *I've done eight years as an operator but I have one story that shocked me a little. I had two years on at the time and was doing an overnight route. I picked up two males who appeared to be intoxicated, an elderly lady and a young teen. I was driving through the route when I heard a gasp from the elderly lady. She came up to me as I was driving and said: "This is very disgusting. Please let me off." I had no idea what she was talking about until I looked back and saw one of the males at the back of the bus performing oral sex on the other man. I had to deal with it on the spot and they complied. I don't care what people do with each other but on a public transit system* *there has to be some sort of public etiquette. It is public transit not private transit.*

Operator 29: *I am a female operator so I tend to be overly cautious when I do the late shifts because you just never know who is going to get on the vehicle. The strangest thing happened to me one time while I was driving the streetcar during the evening rush hour. As the vehicle got full, there was a man who stood right beside me. Looked like a normal man to me so I didn't pay much attention to him. When the streetcar was emptying out due to being at the last stop, the same man who stood beside me reached around the barrier and try to touch my face. He said I was cute and how he wanted to touch me. I was appalled and felt that my space was violated and after expressing my concerns and objections towards the man he left the vehicle. I can only imagine what the man would try if there wasn't a barrier between him and me. Who knows what he would try to do.*

Operator 30: *I remember when I was operating my bus and this was before the barriers were installed by the TTC. A man walked over to the driver's area and put his hand on my leg and said he wanted to perform oral sex on me. I was totally shocked and I pulled his arm away from my leg, stopped the bus and immediately told him to leave the bus. After he left I was visibly shaken because I never knew such things could happen so blatantly.*

Operator 31: *Half way through my shift, driving in the late evening, I only had one male passenger and I thought it was going* to be a very quiet shift for me. I usually have my barrier up during the night time just because I am a female and it is for my personal protection. The passenger stop called cord was pulled and the man walked up to the front and reached around the barrier and touched my breast. He then proceeded to ask for my number so he could call me. I didn't expect what he did at all and I was frozen in my seat and started to tear up. He exited the vehicle as he realized through my reaction how devastated I was.

Operator 32: I am not afraid of being touched or sexually assaulted because I realize on this job that you can't look sexy or show any inclination of interest to anyone. I haven't had any guy touch me but I have had guys give me their numbers and go as far as to stalk me when I drive on different routes. You just have to be really careful when you are working in the public environment.

Operator 33: I'm doing the 506 Carlton streetcar. I am pulling in the Howard Park loop and I only have two people with me onboard. There was an Asian man and a small boy, probably around 4 or 5 years old, a very cute kid. They get off the streetcar and I get off my seat to change the destination sign and set my transfer to the right time. I look up and see the man taking a picture. No big deal lots of tourist do that, so I think nothing of it. I close the front doors, ready to power off and wave back at the man but I only see the man and no kid. I look at where the sandbox is to see if he is hiding around it since he was a very small kid, but don't see him. The man is still taking pictures but at this time I don't like the fact that I don't see the kid. I *check my mirrors and still no kid. Now I fully secure the streetcar and lean over to where the front of the streetcar is and there I see the little boy posing for his father and the camera. He was so small that the front mirrors don't get his image, but I could have killed the little boy. I can honestly say that I was a little shaken when I realized the possibilities of that accident became real but thankfully I'm always aware of my surroundings. TTC operators I would say are amazing drivers because of the many dangers we see and face on a daily basis.*

Operator 34: *Being a TTC operator made me an excellent driver. As a matter of fact sometimes my wife hates it when I am in the passenger seat because I tend to point out all the potential dangers that I see, way before she sees them. But there are so many things that can pose a threat to the livelihood of myself and the passengers onboard.*

Operator 35: *During my first year as an operator Ii didn't realize how stressed I would become and how anxious I would be because of the amount of stuff that we actually go through. The shifts, the people, the conditions of the road, it was getting to me. I had to go for counselling just to release the stress that I was dealing with. It is not an easy job mentally, and it's definitely not for everyone.*

Operator 36: *One of the toughest things to deal with is when people don't have the proper fares. It happens every day. Rarely do you find someone who doesn't have the right fare but remembers you another time and pays you what they owe. I do often give the people the benefit of the doubt.*

Sometimes they don't remember to pay when they see me next; sometimes they have the right fare in their hands and really want to see if they can get away with it. So I give them a ride not knowing if the customer is telling the truth about not having the proper fare. There was a young man who had a job interview that day but had no money to pay the fare. He stated that he would pay by the end of the week . Every day I saw the same man and everyday he said he had no money and would pay by the end of the week. I actually was entertained by this because I really wanted to see if he would be a man of his word and pay at the end of the week. The end of the week came and the man came on the bus with a full smile and said: "I told you I would pay you by the end of the week." And he put $60 in the fare box. That actually touched my heart seeing what this young man did. He kept his word and this rarely happens.

Operator 37: *One day I was driving on the route that was heading to Union Station. Coming to a stop I saw a man in business attire, perhaps going to a meeting. He boarded and asked me if the bus went to Union. I replied 'yes'. He was about to walk towards the back of the bus without paying, so I motioned to him with my hand and pointed at the fare box. He then went to the fare box and put his mouth to it and said: "Union Station, please." I laughed a little and said to him: "I don't think it heard you." I explained to him that the fare box doesn't talk back. Afterwards, we both had a good laugh about it.*

Operator 38: *You know all of us (TTC operators) have many stories. It is amazing that we get to share them. I remember when*

I was driving on Parliament going northbound, a lady got on my bus, paid her fare and sat down. Two hours later I picked up the same lady with the same transfer and I explained to her the rules about the transfer. She told me that an another operator told her to use this transfer to go back to her destination because she got off at the wrong stop. I advised her that I was the operator who issued the transfer to her. Her face turned all red and she said: "You got me." And she paid her fare and sat down.

Operator 39:   *A lady got on my bus. From her outward appearance she looked very well off, having fancy clothes, carrying a small dog in her arms and she spoke very eloquently. She quietly said to me as she entered that all she had was a $20 bill and she showed it to me. I gave her a little speech about the fare and said that next time she should have it. She thanked me and I continued driving. As I was driving I heard a bag of some sort hitting the floor as I came to a stop at the light. I secured the bus to make sure that no one was hurt and I saw the same lady picking up loonies and toonies from the floor. She looked up and saw me looking at her in a state of confusion and she slowly came back up to the fare box and dropped in the proper fare. I had to chuckle to myself about the way she tried to deceive me. It bit her back.*

Operator 40:   *Twenty-nine years on the job and there are so many stories that I have that I forgotten now. I have no regrets though working for TTC. You hear some operators complain and complain but really don't see how tough it is out there to get a job. I know it can be hard with the public and deal-*

ing with difficult customers. I guess you have to develop a thick skin as an operator but at the same time you can't let things that are out of your control get a hold of you.

Operator 41: It is hard to hang around at the divisions because all you hear is negative talk from operators. It would literally bring down my spirit. I know that everyone has a bad day here or there but not every day. Some operators don't know how good they have it with the TTC.

Operator 42: I believe people can tell whether you are in a good mood or bad mood and I tend to give out that positive energy when I'm working. I have passengers on a daily basis say thank you to me but I hear there are other operators who have issues on a daily basis. I don't know why that happens to others and not me, but I really tend to always smile despite what is happening on the road or the volume of passengers on my vehicle.

Operator 43: One of the things that operators don't realize is that you really need to have a life outside of the TTC. I've done 30 years and there are guys who work every day, trying to get as much overtime as possible but when they retire they have no life. I think because of the long shifts and the splits, being an operator is how they define themselves. This job can literally destroy your life and your body if you don't have other hobbies on the side.

Operator 44: I worked for over three months straight once and I would say the reason was because I had nothing else to do. Over time friends leave you and even the connection with your *family starts to go down a little. The shifts make it hard to maintain a healthy social life.*

Operator 45: *The reason why I work so much is because I literally see myself as an operator. I know that sounds bad but I know it would be so hard for me to retire because all I know is being a TTC driver.*

Operator 46: *The thing about the TTC and why it is such a great company is the fact that there are so many jobs to pursue and to go for. It is literally up to the employee to pursue whatever is available within the company.*

Operator 47: *I have been an operator for 20 years and I love being an operator. The reason why I didn't want to go after other positions was because at the time I had to deal with my family. I guess when my family got older and more stable, I was getting better and better shifts and so I stayed an operator. But the TTC offers so many opportunities but most stay where they are because of the fear of the unknown.*

Operator 48: *Personally I would say that for a lot of operators, their whole life is just being an operator. They strive for money, and want to be the enforcers of fares and just think that the TTC vehicles belong to them. There is a difference between taking pride in what you do and just overdoing it. When you overdo it of course the passengers are going to react in anger. For instance, I know personally of an operator who would not let anyone on even though it was freezing outside if they didn't have the right fare. I mean*

I understand about the business aspect of the job, but where's the heart?

Operator 49: *Well, I must be very honest. I have no problems at all with this company or the public. Zero absences, zero complaints, have never missed a day at work. I simply come to work and go home. I enjoy what I do but it is not my life and I am not a troublemaker. I am very grateful for this job and wouldn't do anything to jeopardize it.*

Operator 50: *I have three years on the job at the present time and I have had many things happen to me at work. One in particular does come to mind though, and the customer and I had a great laugh about it afterwards. I stopped and opened the vehicle door and a beautiful woman ran on all hysterical and crying because she left her cellphone on one of the streetcars. I gathered some info from her regarding the cellphone and called my supervisor so that a message could be sent out to the all the streetcars on that route to look out for the cellphone. She was panicking and as the message was sent out to the streetcars, she immediately stopped crying and realized that she had left her phone plugged in at a Thai restaurant. Needless to say we had a chuckle and off she went.*

Operator 51: *I only have five years on but it seems like I have over 20 years' experience with the amount of things that have happened to me. I remember one story and I think this is probably the best one. I picked up two guys late at night and it was so late that they were the only ones on the vehicle. I told them not to smoke on the vehicle* *because when I picked them up they were still smoking and just quickly put out the cigarettes. They complied and said that they wouldn't smoke. While driving, from time to time I like to look at my mirrors to always be careful and vigilant with my surroundings. When I looked at my interior mirrors I thought it was foggy and thought nothing about it because it was raining a little. I kept on looking at my mirrors and thought it was strange that the outside mirrors and the front dash weren't getting foggy at all. It was just the interior side mirrors. When the streetcar was stopped and secure I went to wipe my mirror and then saw it wasn't fogged up at all but it was the smoke created by the two men who came on the streetcar. I looked back and saw a cloud of smoke at the back where those two guys were sat, and it wasn't cigarettes that they were smoking. Needless to say I got them off the vehicle. The overnight service and the daytime service that the TTC offers are literally opposite extremes. So much goes on during the night, it is like a whole different Toronto.*

Operator 52: *I have had a drunken couple at the back of the vehicle making out so much that it disgusted the people around them. By the time I looked back they were fully involved in a sexual act, only for a moment and then they left.*

Operator 53: *When I got to the end of my route I had a little extra time before beginning the trip back. Walking to the back of the vehicle I smelt this odour and it was very strong the closer I got. As I got to the back I looked down and saw one seat of the vehicle covered in urine. The smell was very repulsive.*

Operator 54: *I had an experience once when a teen girl driving a very nice car hit the side of my bus and her car was crushed. She was drunk and had just left her friend's place. Within a few minutes another car drove up to the scene of the accident, a guy got out and literally walked over to me and took out his wallet. It was around 2:00 am and as he took out his wallet, cash spewed out everywhere. He took out at least $4000 and told me that the money was mine if I don't call the police and I just let the girl go.*

Operator 55: *Here come all these guys and girls dressed in their suits and dresses getting onto my vehicle. I guess these kids were going to prom but they didn't have money for a limousine. They all got on and this drunk man got on after them and just started to cause trouble. The drunk man was waving at the girls and cussing at the guys. I was fairly new so I was getting a little nervous. Before long one of the guys asked me to open the back door, so I did. All I saw was the drunk man flying out of the back doors.*

Operator 56: *I know that the TTC accepts everyone and anyone, since we live in such a diverse city, with all the different cultures, it is beautiful to see such a mix. However on a hot and very humid day, I remember my co-worker getting off the bus and warning me about a man on the bus who had a very bad odour coming from him. I didn't pay any attention to him, and probably assumed that he was only joking around. I got on the bus to organize my working space and then I noticed that all the passengers were sitting cramped at the back of the bus away from this one* *man who smelled so bad. I had to drive with this strong odour for about 30 minutes and I couldn't say anything.*

Operator 57: *I was driving the bus on a very cold night. I came to a stop and lowered the bus and was about to proceed forward when I felt the whole bus jerk forward. It was unusual so I decided to check the bus from outside to see what happened. To my amazement, a car had driven right into the back of the bus and the teens that were driving the car were trying to leave the scene. I remember seeing them frantically panicking and trying to reverse their car away from the bus. One of the two got out of the car and asked me not to report it or call the cops because they didn't have insurance. Luckily the cops were driving by and stopped just before the teenagers could flee the scene. Sometimes even when operators least expect it they can be put into a compromising position. Who knew what those kids had on them if I had said that I wouldn't comply with their suggestion.*

Operator 58: *I had one gentleman ask me for a location that I really didn't know because I was new to that route. He became so rude and started to belittle me in front of all the passengers. I asked him where he worked and he responded "at an office building." I asked him what floor and he stated the floor number. I asked him if he knew what was going on at a different floor. He stated no and walked away.*

Operator 59: *I have a story that made me feel like a criminal. A person was driving their car on the right side of the streetcar and* *was angry because he obviously felt that I wasn't letting him pass. So every time he got close to where he could see me he would wind down his window and give me the finger. I didn't pay any attention to him and I believe that this angered him even more. He accelerated, cut in front of the streetcar and stopped. Well inevitably I reacted by slamming on the brakes but made contact with his vehicle.*

Operator 60: *The amount of frustrated passengers increases especially when there are delays in their journeys and frustration breeds contempt. There was an issue with the subway which resulted in everyone on that particular train having to exit the subway and wait upstairs for the shuttle buses to come. I was at the end of my shift and was on my way to return the bus to my home division. I was requested to help out with the shuttle buses and I agreed. When I got to the station and saw the station just full of angry passengers and all they saw was one bus coming which was mine. When I got to the platform and opened the doors for them to board, all I heard were complaints about how much the TTC sucks, and how I was late and why I took so long to come. I literally felt so low and degraded. I could have been home with my wife and kids but here I was helping out. It is a shame that the public doesn't realize the sacrifice that TTC operators make sometimes in order to service the city of Toronto.*

Vision is not enough. It must be combined with venture. It is not enough to stare up the steps, we must step up the stairs.

—Vaclav Havel

CHAPTER 8

———

SO WHAT NOW?

s it possible to change the way that the public views the TTC
and more importantly its frontline workers? Is it possible to move
towards an understanding between the public and the operators? I believe without a shadow of doubt that it is possible, that
the public can get a better understanding about the dangers transit
operators face and the sacrifices they make in to serve the city and
people of Toronto. Through both my own story and those of other TTC operators, it is clear how the way passengers treat operators, good or bad, has a profound effect on the individuals involved.
It is clear how having to deal day in and day out with disrespectful
passengers can lead to depression, relationship breakdowns and
feelings of inadequacy on the job. So is there a proper course of
action to be taken by those who rely on the transit on a daily basis?

Call To Action: Passengers

The proper course of action for the passengers is to consider saying
these two simple phrases: "please" and "thank you." These small

yet powerful words can soften the hardest heart, and transform a frowning face into a smiling one.

> *Make it a habit to tell people thank you. To express*
> *your appreciation, sincerely and without anything in return.*
> *Truly appreciate those around you, and you'll soon find*
> *many others around you. Truly appreciate life,*
> *and you'll find that you have more of it.*
> —Ralph Marston

I remember returning to Toronto after a week's vacation one time. I was on the plane and the passengers clapped and cheered for the excellent job that the crew and pilot did when the plane landed. Looking over to my friend, I said how amazing it was that the passengers were so thankful when the pilot flew the plane and brought them to their destination safe and sound. The staff were just doing their job correctly. It made me think of the TTC operators and transit operators around the world. Perhaps on a smaller scale but we do the same thing: perform our duties in a safe and secure manner to get everyone to their destination. Yet for the majority of the public, they'd rather complain and abuse than show any appreciation. I'm not saying that there should be outbursts of applause every time you get to the end of the bus route or the subway line, but to not even acknowledge the very existence of the individual who brought you to your destination safely is not right either. So a "hi", "thank you", "please" would go a long way for the TTC operator, I'm sure of it.

Imagine having a community of grateful passengers and humbled operators working together in serving each other. What a transit system that would be! So I send out a challenge to you. If you use the transit system regularly, perform an act of kindness once a day towards a bus driver, streetcar operator or subway operator who got you to your destination safely and on time. I challenge you no matter what the circumstances. You could be the only channel of positive energy that the operator receives for that whole day.

Toronto is the largest city in Canada and, according to *The Economist*, Toronto is one of the best cities in the world to live in. Let us lead by example with the way that we treat each other during our commutes. There needs to be a change in understanding between how the public at large see the frontline workers of the TTC. TTC operators are every bit as human as the passengers on the vehicles. They eat, they sleep, they work, they feel pain, sorrow and joy. TTC operators deserve to be treated with the same respect as your family, friends, colleagues or your boss.

Don't get me wrong. On every apple tree there are good apples and bad apples. It's the same with frontline workers. There are some who give off negative energy but why not counter that frown with your own positive energy? Why not return a rude comment or even a delay in the route or a late vehicle with saying those two magical words: "Thank you." Gratitude is the agent of change.

But this goes beyond just the fair treatment of operators and extends to the fair treatment of other passengers on the transit system with you. How many times have you seen someone sitting in a priority seating area (seats that are for the elderly, pregnant women and people with disabilities) and all along there is someone who really needs those seats standing up close by? How many times have you heard someone on the phone talking so loudly that it literally disturbs everyone on the vehicle? Recently there was a newspaper article that perfectly illustrates the type of behavioural etiquette that needs to be shown when using public transit.

February 2015, The Panther Press

Opinions

Transit Etiquette

Respectfully Travelling on the TTC

January 8, 2015

Jareeat Purnava

1. *Say "excuse me" when you're trying to get to the door. Most of the time, the bus is so crammed it can only be described as a can of sardines, so it's natural to want to push past people to get to the door …*

2. *Give up your seats for the elderly, pregnant, and the disabled … It's up to you to notice when others need a seat and then offer your own respectfully.*

3. *When the bus driver says to move to the back, please, move to the back.*

4. *In a quiet bus, don't talk too loudly. It's disturbing to others (much like a library), and causes a bit of an embarrassment for yourself.*

5. *Don't disturb the driver without a reason. Looking for directions? Trying to figure out if you got on the wrong bus? The bus driver is there to help you, but be really careful not to distract him/her. Try asking your question when the bus stops.*

Remember, this is public transit. You are sharing the space with strangers so it's very important to be polite and respectful. Continue commuting respectfully.

One of the things I have difficulty understanding is the absence of compassion in the hearts of some when it comes to the transit system. We all have seen people rush on the vehicles, pushing and shoving in order to get to a seat. This should never be. If you're a passenger, I challenge you to treat everyone with respect, not only the TTC operator but also your fellow passengers.

There is one other issue that needs to be talked about and that is those passengers who on a constant basis try to scam the system by not paying the proper fare and giving many excuses for not paying. The majority of the TTC operators would actually be more lenient if you came and were humble about it and said that you didn't have the adequate funds. But those who scam the system spend more time trying to get away from paying rather than being honest. Let there be an atmosphere of accountability for the actions of the passengers.

Having said all this, I just want to thank those passengers who have been nothing but model citizens and who have displayed kindness towards the operators and other customers. I want to thank those who have given up their seats to the elderly and those in need of priority seating. I want to thank those who consciously turn down their headphones in order to not disturb others. I want to thank those who pay their fares and haven't tried to scam the TTC. I want to thank passengers for their commitment to the TTC and the transit system. There are amazing passengers out there who love the TTC and understand the difficulties that it faces every day. I commend you, all the good and loyal passengers. Without you there is no transit system.

Call To Action: TTC Operators

Speaking from experience as one who walks in the shoes of an operator regularly, dealing with the public has its positive and negative aspects. However, we are in the business of customer service and it is our duty to treat each customer with fairness and kindness.

A story always comes to mind when I think about kindness and going the extra mile for people. I was driving the bus when an elderly woman exited. As she got off the bus she indicated that she wanted to use the crosswalk to get to the other side of the street. In her hands were grocery bags and she appeared to be struggling with them. I was thinking how I wished that someone would help her with her groceries. And then a man appeared on the other side of the street. He was elderly also but that didn't stop him from helping the lady with her groceries. After retrieving the bags, he also struggled to carry them. But the fact that he would go out of his way to help her, when he wasn't very strong himself, really touched my heart.

So, to my fellow operators, we have the ability to touch hundreds of people's lives every day when we put on the TTC uniform. We have the ability to influence, for the better, and to go that extra mile to express kindness to passengers. I have heard complaints from passengers about the mistreatment that they sometimes experience riding the TTC. Hearing about operators leaving people at the stop just to get an extra minute or two at the end of the line makes me sad. I have heard operators answering questions from passengers (who really don't know the system properly or their way around) with a rude and condescending tone. Then there are operators who deliberately play games on the route in order to avoid picking up customers.

But I have a question to ask these operators: Would you treat the passenger in that manner if the CEO was observing you on your shift? Would you dare to leave the end terminal early in order to avoid picking up passengers if the CEO was standing beside you? We have an obligation as the face of the TTC to conduct ourselves in a professional manner, to look professional and to speak professionally. No one is responsible for the way that we treat others, only ourselves. I know there are days when you just don't want to be bothered. I've been there. But we are in the public eye and, like it or not, this is the job that we signed up for.

The TTC doesn't owe you anything. I hope that I don't sound too harsh, but there shouldn't be this sense of entitlement from the operators towards the TTC. They didn't force you into working for them and they are not forcing you to stay. You chose to stay and work for the TTC and despite what people say this is one of the best companies to work for. It just all depends on the attitude that is in your heart towards your job and towards the people that we serve.

I challenge my fellow operators to be a channel of positivity to the supervisors and management, to your colleagues and to the passengers that use the system on a daily basis. I challenge you to give a nice smile to those who come onto the vehicles. Would it be that difficult to go the extra mile and not expect anything in return from the TTC or from the passengers? Take your job seriously and be proud of your work. Many of you do, and the challenge then is to build a culture that is contagious throughout the whole transit system.

Let us not forget the line of work that we are involved in and how fortunate we truly are to work for a great company. We have all sorts of opportunities and career advancements ahead if we work hard. There are countless stories about employees that start at an entry level and grow within the company furthering their careers at a fast pace. There are stories of those who started as operators and then became managers, supervisors, and even moved into executive roles. There are also those who love doing what they are doing as a frontline worker and wouldn't have it any other way. Whatever the desire of the individual, the TTC provides ample opportunity to explore it. We must never forget the privilege that we have by being able to say: "I work for the TTC."

I want to thank the operators in all the bus divisions, the operators in all the subway divisions, and the operators in the streetcar divisions. You have done an amazing job, day in and day out, and Toronto wouldn't be the same without your efforts. I want to actually give out a special thank you to all the operators and staff in the "Wheel Trans" department. These operators transport the elderly and people with disabilities. Often, they get overlooked, but their service is vital. To the TTC employees who have retired—you have paved the way for others. Your years of service and dedication to the TTC must not be forgotten. To those who have passed away, your memory will always live on.

Call To Action: Potential TTC Frontline Workers

So you want to become a TTC operator? You've heard about the benefits and the salary that operators get and that has sparked your interest? There is more to being an operator than just the perks. The job comes with a price. It requires sacrifice, self-control and strong character. Are you willing to work on holidays? Are you willing to work nights and long days because of split shifts? Are you willing to conduct yourself in a manner that would honour the TTC even when a passenger becomes unruly? Unfortunately you will need to develop a thick skin quickly because dealing with the public is not easy and not everyone will understand and respect you.

The Toronto Transit Commission carries approximately 525 million customers per year. That's 1.6 million passengers on a typical weekday. The ridership consists of more than 75% of all transit ridership in the Greater Toronto Area. The TTC operates the third-most heavily used urban transit system in North America, after the New York City Transit Authority and Mexico City Metro. Not every customer is going to be happy and joyful all the time. There are going to be rude ones and those who don't really care what answers you have or what explanations you give to them. There are going to be good and bad experiences due to the fact that not everyone comes from the same ethnic background, speaks the same language, or grew up in the same society. Are you willing to keep your mouth closed and act professionally?

What about the shifts? Are you willing to work hours that are not like those of your friends and family? Knowing that the shifts that you work will affect your friendships, your family life and your social life, are you willing to make such a sacrifice in order to serve Toronto? What if you are married? Do you understand that the TTC has arguably the highest marital divorce rate amongst the public sector? Shift work does affect married life and there are some marriages that crumble while others thrive.

Despite this, I believe that the TTC is one of the greatest companies to work for and, if you have a desire to join them, that's admirable. As you pursue your career with the TTC, give it your all and make not only Toronto but also the TTC proud. You might have much to offer; you might make a difference. So, if you are successful in your pursuit of a TTC frontline worker position, take a tip from me: put a smile on your face and act grateful. It's all you need.

Don't let one day go by without you saying thank you to someone who did something for you. Who knows, those two little words might change a person's life for the better.

—Richard Lee

About The Author

Richard Lee is a vibrant and passionate young man who began trusting his natural gift for storytelling in his late twenties and this has led to his first book. Years of drive and dedication along with the fear of only ever being an "average man" have helped him to become a supervisor today with the Toronto Transit Commission, one of the world's largest transit systems.

MIX
Paper from
responsible sources
FSC® C100212
FSC
www.fsc.org

Printed in August 2015
by Gauvin Press,
Gatineau, Québec